THE NEWER SPIRIT
A SOCIOLOGICAL CRITICISM OF
LITERATURE

THE
NEWER SPIRIT
A SOCIOLOGICAL CRITICISM OF LITERATURE

V. F. CALVERTON
EDITOR, THE MODERN QUARTERLY

INTRODUCTION BY
ERNEST BOYD

OCTAGON BOOKS

A DIVISION OF FARRAR, STRAUS AND GIROUX

New York   1974

Reprinted 1974
by special arrangement with Margo Ann Solin

OCTAGON BOOKS
A DIVISION OF FARRAR, STRAUS & GIROUX, INC.
19 Union Square West
New York, N. Y. 10003

\35729

Library of Congress Cataloging in Publication Data

Calverton, Victor Francis, 1900-
    The newer spirit; a sociological criticism of literature.

    Reprint of the ed. published by Boni & Liveright, New York.

    1. Criticism.   2. Literature—History and criticism.   I. Title.
PN81.C25   1974   801'.95   74-6230
ISBN 0-374-91246-7

Printed in USA by
Thomson-Shore, Inc.
Dexter, Michigan

To

MANON

WITHOUT WHOM THIS BOOK COULD NOT HAVE BEEN

PREFACE

THESE essays are devoted to criticism, which, in these parlous times of mystical illusion and caprice, the author is so bold as to call a science. It is the hope that they will help to clarify the critical approach. Through all of the essays, despite the different fields they explore, there is a continuity of thought and a similarity of analysis.

The reader will have to forgive certain repetitions in several of the studies because they were prepared for publication in different periodicals, and in order that the author's theory should not be misunderstood, or caught only in snatches, it was necessary in a few instances to repeat the fundamental propositions.

If these essays succeed in emphasizing and portraying with convincing vividness the indisseverable relationship of art to life, and the seldom recognized but determining factors in society that create and shape artistic tendencies and expression, they will have achieved their purpose.

V. F. C.

CONTENTS

INTRODUCTION

CRITICISM in America has fallen so inevitably into two classes, the moralizing and the pseudo-æsthetic, that Mr. Calverton's reminder of an element which both overlook is a challenge, and all challenge is valuable. "Although revolutions in esthetics are due to revolutions in ideas, every revolution in ideas is a consequence of a revolution in the social structure that the prevailing material conditions have produced." These words at the close of his essay admirably sum up a thesis which he has developed very effectively in this compact summary of the evolution in literature from the aristocratic ideas of feudalism to the rise of the middle-class, and finally the proletariat—the last two marking off modern from classical literature.

Mr. Calverton's insistence upon the sociological factor in criticism, as I have said, has the value of a challenge, although he perhaps would claim more for it. It is a challenge to the moralizers, for they, I fancy, labour under the delusion that their peculiar prepossessions, their indifference to æsthetics, fulfill to some degree the function of sociological criticism, which must take account of the prevailing social tendencies at the time and place where a work of art or literature is produced. Hence the affecting notion of Professor Stuart Sherman that "beauty has a heart full of service," with its disconcerting corollary as embodied in that author's pamphlet on *The Significance of Sinclair Lewis,* that *Main Street* is to be mentioned in the same category as *Madame Bovary,* and has the advantage over Flaubert's novel of not making "the specific erotic passion" the center of its theme. This sort of thing is what passes currently for literary criticism with a more serious basis than mere esthetics. It reaches its logical culmination in a recent statement by Mr. Walter Prichard Eaton that a play entitled *The Potters,* which enjoyed a considerable vogue during the past season in New York, is superior to *Les Ratés,* by H. R. Lenormand, one of the few younger French dramatists of real distinction, which was produced by the Theater Guild under the title of *The Failures.* Mr. Eaton's reason for this judgment is that everybody has seen people like the Potter family, and witnessed such a scene in the crowded street car as was shown on the stage, whereas none of us ever knew an author who toured the French provinces with his wife, allowed her to keep him on her earnings as a prostitute, and then killed her. Obviously, Cervantes is vastly inferior to Zane Grey, on the same principle, for we all have seen a cowboy, but who ever saw a knight in armour rescuing distressed maidens and tilting at windmills?

I need not multiply instances of this peculiar sort of irrelevancy which is the stock-in-trade of those critics who profess to be concerned with values other than the esthetic. Mr. Calverton's outline of the influences which determine literary forms has the virtue of showing what those factors really are for which the moralists and the professors so calmly substitute their own predilections and superstitions. The phenomena in contemporary American literature which distress the Ku Kluxers of criticism are as inevitable as the phenomena which distressed the classicists when they were confronted with a literature in which the sufferings and struggles of common people were treated as though they had been the sufferings and struggles of kings and princes. Theodore Dreiser and Sherwood Anderson as inevitably reflect America today as Racine the France of Louis XIV. If either of them were to write of America as if it were the America of Hawthorne, he would be as guilty of anachronism as Flaubert would have been, had he described Rouen as his great Norman predecessor Corneille knew it, instead of the Rouen of his own time.

At the same time Mr. Calverton's thesis challenges those whom I have called the pseudo-esthetes, for they try to advance an esthetic *in vacuo*, bearing no relation to the conditions of life in this country. They think that a revolution in ideas will produce a revolution in esthetics. They forget, in Mr. Calverton's phrase, that "every revolution in ideas is a consequence of a revolution in the social structure that the prevailing material conditions have produced." Forgetting this, they turn their eyes incessantly toward Europe, particularly toward Paris, where the material conditions, in many vital aspects, are entirely dissimilar from those existing here. Since the war this is even more markedly true than before, and Europe has gone through experiences, emotional, intellectual, economic and political, which are not only unknown to this country, but may never be known to it. The assumption that America must pass through the same social and industrial stages of evolution as Europe is merely a reflex action of the radical mind; it has no basis of necessity or even of probability.

The artistic reflection of the troubled state of the European mind, so far as it has expressed itself in a definite and specific art form, is Expressionism. It is significant that Germany and Russia, which have been most fundamentally changed by the course of the last ten years, are the two countries which have made the most postive contributions to Expressionist art and literature. So intimate is the connection between the post-war revolutionary soul and Expressionism, that almost every work of literature cast in this form deals with themes and situations and persons who embody the present upheaval and unrest. The plays of Ernest Toller, Fritz von Unruh, Georg Kaiser and Walter Hasenclever portray the turmoil of a people who have been precipitated out of a social order in which they functioned easily, because they had adapted themselves to its workings and had profited by them, into a social order for which they were unprepared and in which they have not yet succeeded in interesting themselves. They depict characters who are haunted and harried by the nightmare of disaster and the vague hopes of a belated and chaotic humanitarianism. At their worst, they are mere propagandists of pacifism and social democracy. However much this may disappoint those who believe that Expressionism is designed for more disinterested artistic service, it is a fact which strikingly offers an up-to-date illustration of Mr. Calverton's contention. It further explains why Americans borrowing this esthetic can graft it on to nothing that is actually alive and has roots in American soil.

In the circumstances, I welcome these essays by the Editor of THE MODERN QUARTERLY, whose aims it incidentally summarizes. He asks our moralizing pedants and censors to reflect upon the realities of a form of criticism of which they offer an obsolete simula-

crum. He draws the attention of their opponents, the
hyper-esthetic young men, to a vital factor in the development of an esthetic, which they ignore. Consequently, Mr. Calverton has something of importance
to say to both parties in the American critical debate:
to those who say, with the late Anthony Comstock—
though not naïvely—"MORALS, not art," and to those
who say, unconsciously, "Art for Paris' sake," in the
touching belief that they are thereby creating American art for art's sake.

ERNEST BOYD.

THE NEWER SPIRIT
A SOCIOLOGICAL CRITICISM OF LITERATURE

THE NEWER SPIRIT

SOCIOLOGICAL CRITICISM OF LITERATURE

THE time when literature was considered the product of a supernatural afflatus or peculiar impartation of spirit or impulse has disappeared. The passing of this notion has been a very simple and perceptible phenomenon. Explanations and descriptions of it have been legion. The advance of science with its revelations of both sidereal and terrestrial activity, and the consequent decline of other-worldly conceptions, the change from the deductive to the inductive method, created a different attitude toward man and his achievements. The change and progress in thought and science have been an inevitable reflection of the steadily transforming material conditions of present and past centuries. Creative and critical composition, if we must make that division for the moment, have altered both in style and substance with each of the vicissitudes of social evolution. The criteria of excellence have varied with each advancing epoch. Literature of the "impossible" and "improbable" cast, which fascinated one age, suffices but to dull and stupefy another; pictures of court and chivalry, the gilded pageantry of palace and field, the sunny romance of knight and lady, which captivated the imagination of artists and critics of olden centuries, no longer allure. The demand for the inevitable and the real becomes as vital a part of the literary creed as the scientific. The tendencies of art, religion, and science are but the interwoven threads of the social texture.

Theories of scientific criticism urged by Hennequin and J. M. Robertson [1] are no more than the necessary extension of sociological development into the critical realm. The idea of Mr. Mencken that the excellency of an author's writing may depend upon nothing more exalted than the activity of his pylorus, and Mr. W. Huntington Wright's, that literary creation is merely a form of physico-chemical reaction, are likewise similar manifestations of this sociological trend. The application of the biographical method to criticism is but part of this same phase. Taine's progress in the examination of literature as the product of telluric and social environment is no more singular, although more happily significant. All are common, and in no way surprising, expressions of our modern age of industrial and scientific growth. They could be characteristic of no other age.

[1] See Robertson's *New Essays Toward a Critical Method.*

As we continue to cautiously and minutely study the literature of any race or period, then, we eventually discover that all of the theories and concepts, the dicta and shibboleths, of creative and critical effort are but the outgrowths of the social system in which they have their being, and which in turn is the product of the material conditions of the time. This point we shall illustrate at considerable length. Under feudalism, for instance, we shall show that the literary conceptions which prevailed were in consonance with the social structure and did not change until the latter began to alter. In similar manner we shall picture the changes in social environment that brought with them the different literary concepts and tactics of the eighteenth and nineteenth centuries. And finally we shall consider the complex expansion of science and industry during the latter part of the nineteenth and beginning of the twentieth centuries, and its effects upon the form and substance of contemporary literature.

Social classes develop within one another. There is no fixed line of demarcation to determine the precise moment of their birth and extinction. Caused by newly arising conditions, they spring into existence slowly or swiftly according to the nature of the exigency, and for a considerable period are quite overlapping entities. The bourgeois class, for example, was a gradual growth in the very heart of feudal society.

[21]

Developing primarily as a result of the industrial changes circling about the Renaissance: the inventions of gunpowder, [1] printing with movable type, the compass, the manufacture of paper on a large scale, and the extension of commerce with the Orient, it did not become permanently dominant until the disappearance of feudalism, or cause any enduring changes in literature until the beginning of the eighteenth century. That does not mean, as some might suppose, that previous to the eighteenth century, literature was entirely unaffected by its rise, but that the effects were too scattered and incoherent to create a distinct and lasting change of literary trend. In the seventeenth century, for instance, the bourgeois class in England rose in successful rebellion against the nobility, and for eleven years established a government of their own, which was characterized by all the extensions and restrictions of the puritanic bourgeois conceptions of the period. The progress of theatrics was temporarily interrupted, and the mundane in literature was supplanted by the religious. The romantic poetry of the Elizabethans was succeeded by the sombre metaphysical lyrics of Daniel, Breton, Donne and Herbert. The change, however, though sharp, was ephemeral. The Restoration brought with it a swift return to the older conceptions

[1] This, of course, was originally invented by the Chinese, but was first applied to warfare by the Occidentals, who used it in this capacity as early as the battle of Crecy in 1346.

and manners. The recoil, for a time, was virulent and excessive. This bourgeois incursion then, as we shall see, wrought no fundamental and permanent change in esthetic theory or practice. Nevertheless, coming as a consequence of economic difficulties forced upon them by the tyrannic taxation of the king, it furnishes incontestable proof of the rising potency of the bourgeois class at the time. It was not to be until some decades later, however, that its class concepts were to become a steadily ruling element in the social and esthetic consciousness.

The attitude toward tragedy that prevailed throughout the feudal period and continued to persist over much of Europe until the bourgeois revolution of 1789, is interesting and conclusive illustration of this division of class-psychology caused by the existing types of social structure. Since the time of Aristotle, and certainly many years before, though we have no written records to certify it, tragedy has been considered the loftiest form of literary art, and to its construction have been devoted the highest artistic energies of man. The psychological reasons, reduced to their material motives, why tragedy has been conceived in such exalted fashion—which would carry us into the problems of "catharsis," the nature of physiological reaction, universal pessimism, the intellectual ennui of civilization—need not be discussed in this treatise. The presence of the conception is what we are immediately concerned with, and its process of change is what we must subject to analysis.

Feudal society, dependent upon agricultural production, was the necessary outgrowth of the various systems of slavery that preceded it. Its apex, the nobility, was the class that determined and fostered the leading conceptions of the age; the manners of court, the practice of chivalry, the system of judicature, the pursuance of the arts, the metaphysics of the period—all were products of the peculiar agrarian system of production and distribution that then existed. The religious class, in possession of extensive and fertile lands, came in conflict with the nobility only when the latter threatened usurpation of such territory, and in general worked for the perpetuation of the feudal regime. The burghers of the town, as we mentioned earlier in our discussion, became influential only as feudalism started to decline.[2] And these esthetic and ethical concepts which prevailed, and that were but the patent reflections of the character of the reigning class, were defended with sincere and unremitting zeal and justified as "absolute."

There is perhaps no clearer evidence of precisely how the ideas of a community, those of its artists and

[2] The rise of these burghers, in fact, was one of the main causes of the decline of the feudal system, although it in turn was the result of still more underlying material causes.

critics, statesmen and metaphysicians, are determined
by the nature of material conditions, from which arise
the structure of society, than that afforded by the
esthetic concept of tragedy. Until the eighteenth century, when the bourgeois class had acquired sufficient
power to exert a permanent influence upon social conceptions, the attitude towards tragedy was uniformly
feudal and aristocratic. The distinction between
higher and lower drama, tragedy and comedy, throughout the Middle Ages and extending to the decline and
decease of feudalism, was considered by critics as being
fundamentally a distinction of social status. Tragedy
could be concerned only with noble characters—the
illustrious—and to conceive it as being written about
a bourgeois protagonist would have been literary sacrilege. If, for a moment, we consider the writings of
that French classicist, Abbe d'Aubignac (1604-76),
we shall discover an explicit statement of this attitude.
Tragedy, says d'Aubignac, "inheres not in the nature
of the catastrophe but in the rank of persons." The
other French classicists were equally firm in their position. Pellitier, Ronsard, de Laudun, Vauquelin de la
Fresnay, Pelet de la Mesnardière, each supported the
aristocratic theory of tragedy, and wrote as if a deviation from it were an impossibility. Voltaire, a radical
in so many things, and whose death occurred only
eleven years before the bourgeois revolution in France,

[25]

was certain that tragedy required characters elevated above the common level. Even Joubert, in the memorable *Encyclopedie,* declared that tragedy is "the imitation of the lives and speech of heroes, subject by their elevation to passions and catastrophes as well as to the manifestations of virtues, of the most illustrious kind." It must not be forgotten that at the time the *Encyclopedie,* under the organization of Diderot, made pretensions to advance to modernism, unrivaled by any other literary or scientific production. The Italian humanists in no case dissented from the aristocratic theory of tragedy. The German pseudo-classicists, Opitz and Gottsched, the directors of literary taste in Germany during a century and a half, the former during the most of the seventeenth and the latter during the first half of the eighteenth, were in avowed agreement with the classicist attitude. In his *Buch von der Deutschen Poeterey* (1624), Opitz gave the aristocratic interpretation to poetry, and later in *Versuch einer Critische Dichtkunst vor die Deutschen* in 1730, Gottsched continued the same criticism. The following quotation from Opitz, for instance, clearly represents the attitude of these German classicists toward tragedy:

"Tragedy . . . seldom permits the introduction of people of humble or common deeds, because it deals only with royal decrees, murders, despairs, slaughters of fathers and children, fires, incests, wars and rebellions, lamentations, outcries, sighs, and the like. Comedy has to do with ordinary matters and persons; it speaks of weddings, banquets, games, tricks and knaveries of serving men, bragging foot-soldiers, love affairs, frivolity of youth, avarice of old age, match-making, and such things which daily occur among the common people."

Gottsched, in his *Critische Dichtkunst,* expresses in terms no less unequivocal the same sentiment:

"If you wish to make a comedy of your subject, the persons must be citizens; for heroes and princes belong in a tragedy. Tragedy is distinguished from comedy only in this, that, instead of laughter, it tries to arouse wonder, terror and pity; therefore it usually concerns itself with men of birth only, who are conspicuous by their rank, name, and appearance. In an epic, which is the masterpiece of all poetry, the persons must be the most impressive in the world, kings, heroes, and great statesmen, and everything in it must sound majestic, strange and wonderful."

The very titles of certain of the romances and tragedies of the period are an interesting and significant index to its social trend: Bucholz's *Pleasant Romance of the Christian Royal Princes Herculiscus and Herculadisla and their Princely Company* (1659); Ziegler's *The Asiatic Banise, or Bloody but Courageous Pegu, Based on Historic Truth but Covered with the*

Veil of a Pleasing Story of Heroic Love-Adventure (1688); and Lohenstein's *The Magnanimous General Arminius, with his Illustrous Thusnelda, Held up to the German Nobility as an Honourable Example and for Praiseworthy Emulation* (1689).

But do we discover dissenting voices in England at the time?—England to which so many panegyrics of liberty have been dedicated. The attitude of their artists and critics is clear and inflexible. For tragedy only the great can be characters; the "dignity of persons," to employ the phrase of Ben Jonson used in this reference, is a necessity if tragedy is to possess elements of the sublime. Such was the avowed attitude of Stubbes, Puttenham, Gosson, Webbe, and Harrington, the eminent critics in the era of the romantic drama, and no deviation from it is to be noted in the writings of Ben Jonson, whom we quoted above, or any of the Restorationists. Rymer contended that tragedy "required not only what is natural, but what is great (noble) in nature." Both Congreve and Dryden declared in favor of the aristocratic conception of tragedy; in Dryden's words, "tragedy, as we know, is wont to image to us the minds and fortunes of noble persons," and in those of Congreve, tragedy "distinguishes itself from vulgar poetry by the dignity of its characters." Even Oliver Goldsmith, the son of a poor curate, a pale struggling genius acquainted with all of the pain and torture of deprivation, maintained that "the distresses of the mean (the middle and poorer classes) by no means affect us so strongly as the calamities of the great." There is no question, therefore, that the aristocratic conception of tragedy was not an isolated, sporadic phenomenon, but a widespread, generally accepted theory.[3]

The dramas of Shakespeare can be taken as fitting example of application of the feudal concept. There have been many, aside from Tolstoi and Shaw, who have attacked Shakespeare for what they call his narrowness of vision, his bigoted reverence for the aristocracy and blatant contempt for the rabble. We might as well attack Plato for considering soldiers an important class in the state, a class to be studied and promoted, and fighting an art to be developed and practiced—or Aristotle for not condemning slavery, the institution that made it possible for Greece at the time to progress and flourish. These strictures, of course, remain, the environment that produced them notwithstanding. It is the environment, however, that makes them explicable—and inevitable. Shakespeare did nothing more than represent the esthetic conceptions of

[3] For certain data presented in this essay credit must be acknowledged to Kuno Francke's *History of German Literature,* and to some of the literary research of William H. Hudson and Ernest Crosby, each of which authors caught hints of the effects of material conditions but in no fundamental sense attempted to coördinate the facts assembled. The coördination is what is significant.

his period. In weaving every tragedy about the struggles of the noble and the illustrious, he violated no concept of his age. Both the commoner and the bourgeois were subjects of humor and satire, the means of affording comedy to the situation and relaxing tenseness in the drama. The humbler classes, as they were called, appear often under titles themselves ludicrous enough to indicate the nature of their treatment: Quince, the Carpenter; Snug, the Joiner; Starveling, the Tailor; Smooth, the Silkman; Bottom, the Weaver; and Flute, the Bellows-maker. In *A Midsummer Night's Dream,* for instance, most of the trades are ridiculed. In all of Shakespeare's works with but a few exceptions, one in *Richard II,* where we find a loyal servant, another in *Cymbeline,* still another in *King Lear,* several in *Timon of Athens,* one in *A Winter's Tale,* two in *Anthony and Cleopatra*—all servants, shepherds or soldiers, who are pictured as faithful and honest—we find unflattering pictures of both proletarian and tradesman. Of the lower class as a whole, the dramatist is even more satirical. In one place characterized as "hempen-homespuns," another as "the barren sort," in still another as "mechanic slaves, with greasy aprons, rules and hammers"; he goes still further in *Coriolanus* to speak of the "stinking breath of the commoner" and decrying them as "the mutable, rank-scented many," "garlic eaters," "multiplying

[30]

spawn," "worthless peasants," "rude unpolished hinds," all phrases consistent with the aristocratic attitude of the time. In *Hamlet,* Shakespeare laments the seeming rise of the lower strata and declares that "the age has grown so picked, that the toe of the peasant comes so near the heel of the courtier, he galls his kibe." Then in *Henry IV* he sneers at the famous rebellion of Wat Tyler, the "damned commotion," which he describes as coming "in base and abject routs, led on by bloody youth, guarded with rags, and countenanced by beggary." In *Pericles* the dramatist proclaims that "princes are a model, which heaven makes like to itself," and in *Henry VI* he has the Duke of York denounce the "mean-born man," and in *Henry VI* Joan of Arc is made to speak of her "contemptible estate." This material instead of being viewed as disturbing and disappointing should rather be considered as satisfying and convincing to the scientific critic, who studies literature as the product of the material conditions that created the society and all of the appurtenances which were necessary to its literary expression. This reference to Shakespeare was made only because his works so excellently illustrate how the esthetic and ethical ideas of the feudal period were expressed in literature, and stand out in such sharp and striking contrast to the changing conceptions of later centuries.

And from whence could such a conception arise?

The Hegelian idealist with his thesis of the absolute might attempt to explain it as the logical development of the absolute idea. But, to us, this appears ridiculously illogical. Besides, the coördinates of absolutist logic are as maddeningly elusive as the motions of a will-o'-the-wisp. On the other hand, we can readily perceive how such a conception, of necessity, must have arisen from the material conditions that had created the feudal regime. As long as the nobility remained the ruling class, the administering and not the administered, it would be a sociological solecism to expect ideas to be other than reflections of the aristocratic, courtly attitude. In no instance in history do we discover such a solecism. The aristocratic conception of tragedy, therefore, continued as long as feudalism existed, and when the system of feudalism could no longer function—the declining nobility steadily becoming more and more dependent upon the rising bourgeois—and had to recede in favor of another system of more adequate and satisfactory dimensions, the concept faded into a myth. That this process of the decline and disappearance of the aristocratic concept was purely a matter of change of social environment, which at basis was due to the failure of feudalism to adapt itself to the demands of its growing communities, was unquestionably proven by the sequence of "bourgeois" tragedy, concomitant with the ascent of the bourgeois class.

In England feudalism experienced a more rapid retrogression than in any other European country. Due to its peninsular location, which afforded a sense of security and protection, a merchant class was an early historical necessity, and in correspondence with the growth of towns and commerce this class became augmented. In France, for example, where the land was part of the continent, without peninsular advantages or handicaps, the bourgeois class did not revolt until over one hundred and forty years after the bloody revolution of the bourgeois in England. As a consequence, we find bourgeois concepts, political and esthetic, developing in England long before. France, and Voltaire's letters, therefore, appear in no way singular. The political and judicial liberty for which England, in every history, has been so conspicuously noted, then, was ultimately the result of this geographic factor.

In England, it follows, if our logic be correct, we should locate the first deviations from the aristocratic conception. And so we do. The play that is commonly referred to as marking the origin of *tragedie bourgeoise* in England is Lillo's *The London Merchant* which was staged by Theophilus Cibber in 1731. The tragedy of this play is concerned with the moral decay

[33]

and execution of a merchant's apprentice, George
Barnwell, whose end was so dismal because he failed
to live a life of sincerity and rectitude.   In brief, the
play is an encomium of bourgeois virtues made em-
phatic by frequent moral lessons and sharp condemnation of all wayward traits.   This play received more
comment and laudation than perhaps any other play
of the century.   It was acted before crowded audiences, night after night in the heat of midsummer,
and drew the patronage and praise of poet and critic.
Within a few years five authorized editions of it were
printed.   Pope, amid the clamor of court and forum,
gave the tragedy his commendation.   Later the play
won the attention and admiration of Rousseau, Marmontel, Prévost, Lessing, Goethe, Schiller, and the extravagant eulogy of Diderot.   In 1796 its theme was
worked into a novel by Thomas Skinner Surr, and
afterwards memoirs of George Barnwell and a life history were written.   It was acted by a number of famous actors and actresses, among whom were Charles
Kemble, Mrs. Siddons, and Sir Henry Irving.   Considered by our present dramatic standards, *The London
Merchant* is a fifth-rate production.   Its homilies are
ludicrous, its characters, including the merchant
Thorowgood, stilted and unnatural, and its points of
dramatic intensity almost laughably unconvincing.

From a historical standpoint, however, as we have noted, the tragedy is significant.

It is necessary to admit, of course, that *The London Merchant* was not the first tragedy in English which was constructed about bourgeois characters. No social movement can be said to have expressed itself in any single moment or episode; the expression is usually gradual and hints at its coming long before its arrival. In Heywood's *A Woman Killed with Kindness* we have an early suggestion of the rising trend and in Otway's *The Orphan*, Southern's *Fatal Marriage*, and Rowe's *The Fair Penitent* we meet with even more marked evidences of the Domestic Tragedy. Yet none of these tragedies possess the thoroughly bourgeois character of *The London Merchant*, or, for that matter, of the two famous plays that followed Lillo's tragedy: *The Gamester* and *The Mysterious Husband*, and cannot be considered as anything more than mild and minor predecessors.

As the bourgeois class, with the steady decline of feudalism, continued to rise in other countries, the aristocratic conception waned. In Germany, for instance, we find Lessing acting the part of the revolutionist. His play *Miss Sarah Simpson*, which appeared in 1755, was the first German tragedy of bourgeois life. His achievement in this drama was very similar to that of George Lillo in *The London Merchant* and Edward

[35]

Moore in *The Gamester*. This, of course, was a complete departure from the theories of Opitz and Gottsched, and later was explained and justified by Lessing in his critical writings. It is important to observe here that with all of his radical notions as to dramatic theme and technique, and even his attack upon Frederick, he still clung to a kind of nationalist sentiment⁴ that the internationalist of the twentieth century would ridicule. Had industry developed, science grown, commerce expanded, cities enlarged, and intercourse taken on the world-wide aspect of late decades, Lessing, with his other radical characteristics, in turn would have forsaken the tiniest vestige of nationalism. In *Minna von Barnhelm* he devoted him·self to a description of "a people beginning to feel itself again as a whole, and to be again conscious of national responsibilities." It would be illogical, from a sociological viewpoint, to expect Lessing to have been otherwise. In *Emilia Galloti* (1772) he fought against the oppression of the bourgeois by the aristocracy; from the play, according to Francke, can be traced the beginnings of the battles carried on by the *Sturm und Drang* movement. In France, Nivelle de la Chaussée and Diderot were the innovators of the *tragedie bourgeoise,* and later Saurin, the author of *Beverly,* an adaption of Moore's *Gamester,* in the century follow-

⁴ St. 101, Works 7, 474.

ing, extended the *tragedie bourgeoise* to include a wider scope.

So long as the supremacy of the bourgeois remained unquestioned, which was certainly the case until the appearance of the modern utopians,[5] Pierre le Roux, Fourier and Saint Simon, there could be but two kinds of ethical and esthetic conceptions, one dominant, the bourgeois, the other recessive or vestigial, the aristocratic. If we take America during the period immediately following the Revolutionary War, we shall discover a fruitful illustration of the effects of bourgeois ascendency. One would scarcely expect, nor does he find, in a country that has just experienced a triumph of its bourgeois,[6] a literature devoted to the praise either of its aristocracy or its proletariat. In a nation where Madison and Pinckney disagreed as to the three classes for which the Constitution should provide, Madison being in favor of the landed, the commercial, and *· ·* manufacturing, and Pinckney in favor of the professional, the landed, and the commercial, neither believing the proletariat worthy of

[5] Unless we wish to begin with Godwin's *Political Justice* (1793) which, in one sense, can be used as a starting point for the modern utopians.

[6] For information as to the American Revolution's representing a clear victory for the merchant class, the bourgeois, the reader may refer to A. M. Symons' *Social Forces in American History*, or to more orthodox historians and their work, such as Farrand's *Development of the U. S.*, Schlesinger's *Colonial Revolution*, or McMaster's *History of the People of the United States*. Beard, likewise, can be used in this reference, or James Oneal.

consideration, it would be contrary to social evolution to find literary themes revolving about the tragic struggles and tribulations of the proletarian characters. In no work of the period do we see the proletarian accepted as fit character for tragedy, or his adversity pictured in bold but sympathetic line and color. Irving used him as a source of sport and satire, Cooper as a frontiersman to combat his fantastic, rainbow-plumed Indians, and Franklin as suitable object for bourgeois sermons on thrift and wisdom. Neither can the verse of Freneau, Barlow, Hopkinson and Drake, nor the prose of Jefferson, Washington or Brockden Brown be said to have treated him in gentler fashion. In England, as we have described, the proletarian now served as material for wit and comedy. In France and Germany, where de la Chaussée and Lessing had emancipated the stage from the aristocratic conception, the proletarian had to be likewise, by esthetic necessity, subservient to the bourgeois, the ascending class.

In the first stages of capitalism the distinction between the bourgeois and the proletarian is not as wide and definite and not so difficult to bridge as in its later stages, when, through the increase and concentration of its mass, it steadily dispossesses and enlarges its lower element and fortifies and narrows its upper. As this dispossession process continues, unless there be some disturbing and deceptive factor, such as the freeland policy, which we found in America during the nineteenth century, the class-consciousness of the dispossessed class grows in ratio with the degree of dispossession. Until this process has developed and intensified there is no significant class-organization, and without organization a class cannot impress itself upon the activity of a society, or function as a determinant of its basic conceptions. During this period, the incipiency of capitalism, for instance, the bourgeois exercised supreme and unquestioned authority; the first labor unions did not organize in America until about 1805 or 1810, over forty-five years after the beginning of the Industrial Revolution, and their organization approximated nothing extensive or involved until the 60's or 70's. The Haymarket episode, of course, weakened the purpose and temporarily wrecked much of this later complexity of organization. These labor organizations, distinct products of class-consciousness,[7] came as the inevitable result of the increasing concentration of capital. With this steady rise of the proletarian, his organization into a definite class with definite class-interests, and with the acquisition of certain educational privileges necessary to his expression, society was driven into acknowledgment of the reality and importance of his existence, and as a consequence

[7] The swift spread of this class-consciousness was due in good part to the fact that the free-lands in the West had been largely consumed.

he became a force in the molding of social conceptions. James Russell Lowell, despite his miserably inferior *Vision of Sir Launfal* and a number of his classic prejudices, was one of the voices of this trend. In his Birmingham address in 1884, just two years before the Haymarket riot, he revealed how very profoundly the rise of the proletariat had affected his ideas and changed his attitude:

"What is really ominous of danger to the existing order of things is not democracy (which, properly understood, is a conservative force), but the Socialism which may find a fulcrum in it. If we cannot equalize conditions and fortunes any more than we can equalize the brains of men—and a very sagacious person has said that 'where two men ride of a horse, one must ride behind'—we can yet, perhaps, do something to correct these methods and influences that lead to enormous inequalities, and to prevent their growing more enormous. . . . Communism means barbarism, but Socialism means, or wishes to mean, coöperation and community of interests, sympathy, the giving to the hands not so large a share as to the brains, but a larger share than hitherto in the wealth they must combine to produce—means, in short, the practical application of Christianity to life, and has in it the secret of an orderly and benign reconstruction."

Although this is what we should classify as sentimental or utopian socialism, it nevertheless is an interesting reflection of the movement of thought caused by the change in material conditions which brought the proletariat into economical and political significance.

Walt Whitman was a finer product of this trend. Into more genuinely poetic, although more mystical, phraseology did he put its aspirations and dreams. With Whitman we find the proletarian no longer the inferior, the source of sport and travesty, but a being infused with the same elements of power and excellence as the heroic general or statesman, a being capable of the deepest thoughts and feelings, and of the profoundest struggle and tragedy. A little over a century earlier, Whitman—but he would not have been the Walt Whitman we know because he would have been made by different conditions—would have sung of other heroes and embodied in his poetic philosophy nothing of the spirit of the proletarian. Instead of a hymn to *A Common Prostitute* he would have bemoaned the fateful end of a princess, or perhaps the daughter of a Thorowgood, and instead of crying that "no one thing in the universe is inferior to another thing," that "behind each mask was a kindred soul," he would have crooned the songs of a priest or composed madrigals to stupid, courtly dames or romantic and prurient maidens.

It is important at this point to note likewise the indisseverable connection between the nature of literary technique and the stage of development of society. Hitherto we have shown how the social conceptions that prevail determine the substance of literature, but not how the form, the technique, the very manner in which the composition is constructed, is determined also by the same material conditions that created the social conceptions. We shall draw only one parallel, which will prove sufficient evidence to establish the premise. This time, to introduce variety, we shall take the novel for our illustration. The first novels, if we exclude such ollapodrida as Petronius' *Satyricon,* Cervantes' *Don Quixote,*[8] Sidney's *Arcadia,* Mrs. Manley's *The Power of Love, in Seven Novels* (1720), appeared in England during the heyday of bourgeois supremacy. Exactly nine years after the staging of *The London Merchant,* Richardson's *Pamela* was printed.[9] Although *Pamela* was parodied by Fielding in *Joseph Andrews,* and the general spirit of the Richardson novels for a time was satirized also by Smollett and Sterne, it was succeeded by *David Simple* and Goldsmith's *Vicar of Wakefield,* both novels dedicated to a similar exaltation of bourgeois virtues. But we are

[8] Macaulay called *Don Quixote,* which it should be remembered appeared quite a number of years before *Pamela,* "certainly the best novel in the world beyond all comparison."

[9] It is curious to note also that in France Marivaux's novel *Marianne,* based upon similar plot and purpose, was published several years earlier than *Pamela.*

not concerned here with an analysis of the substance of the novel, as we were in the case of the drama, but with its form, which renders further dissection of content at this point entirely superfluous.

The more carefully we notice the history of fiction, and the novel need only serve as one instance, we are immediately impressed by the evolution from the impossible to the improbable, thence to the probable and finally to the inevitable. To many, even to the American critic, we dare say, who first recorded this feature, this evolution seems a quite unaccountable affair. That the mythical, legendary romances of Arthur and the Round Table should have prevailed in the four or five centuries following the Norman Conquest, and finally been crystallized into the memorable *Morte d'Arthur* in 1485, all "impossible" in content, is nothing strange nor unexpected to the scientific critic. The fierce encounters of knights, with the perilous enemies of the forest, giants, dragons, mystical swords that could be drawn only with an enchanting sign or whisper, charms evoked by the wicked sorcery of medieval magicians, made up the category of fascinating "impossibilities." *The Castle of Otranto, The Champion of Virtue*, Matthew Lewis' *The Monk*, the weird stories of Mrs. Radcliffe, even Godwin's *St. Leon*, can be classified also in the "impossible" group. The romance of castle and field, which was carried on in the tragedies of the Elizabethans and all of the seventeenth and early eighteenth century dramatists, under more realistic and convincing guise, marked the advance to the improbable and probable stage. The nineteenth century, for instance, was the century for the "probable" in fiction, although the grotesque tales of Poe and Hoffmann are clear evidence of the survival of the improbable and even a phase of the impossible trend. Romantic fiction is all a vestige of these older trends, each produced by different stages of social structure. That certain of these trends should persist after the social environment that caused them has declined and disappeared does not mean that a surprising or confusing element has been introduced into the historical process. It would be surprising and confusing if such remnants of the old ideology did not from time to time spring into print. By our very knowledge of the law of cause and effect we can easily see that the advance of a new social system though it achieved a change in the dominant esthetic and ethical ideas cannot hope to annihilate at once, or in a generation or two, all of the remains of those conceptions that have been forced to recede into the background. There are still royalists in France, although political democracy has been almost a universally accepted theory in the countries of the civilized world.

It was not until science advanced into its later stages,

when the reactions of the mind and body as well as those of matter came to be recognized as following the same inescapable law of cause and effect, that the idea of the inevitable could assume scientific form. Prediction, the aim of science, now became possible in mental as well as physical things, and the causal law attained the extensions necessary to undermine beliefs in chance and the fortuitous. Without the rise of science, which was part of the development of the capitalist system, the idea of the inevitable would never have emerged from its religious raiment, and esthetic conceptions would have been but scantily affected by its existence. At the time that prose and poetic fiction possessed the impossible and improbable cast, the human mind, ignorant of natural law and scientific generalization, demanded nothing more of its literary substance; when knowledge advanced, however, and reality began to be sifted from myth, the literary form became modified in accordance with the nature of the advance. In pace with the progress of science, therefore, did metamorphosis in literary practice result. At the present time, the twentieth century, and also during the latter part of the nineteenth, particularly after the appearance of *The History of Civilization in England, The Origin of Species* and *Das Kapital,* realism of the inevitable character developed. The realism of Sterne, Smollett, and even Fielding, was not the realism that the nineteenth and twentieth centuries require; the former was more plastic, yielding, without the quality of the inevitable, the undeviating necessity, such as we find exemplified in the novels of Hardy and Conrad. The inflexible criterion of modern realism is "inevitability." Situations must flow inevitably from each other; characters must perform only those actions which, in the nature of their being, it was impossible for them not to perform. There must be no appeal to mere possibility or probability if the fiction is to convince. Although the large category of so-called popular magazines of the amorous, snappy and adventurous variety, with which every civilized country is flooded, and the Wrightian and Corellian novels, still cling to the improbable and probable types—hence their success as investments, but failures as literature—there is not a single significant literary periodical or author that would dare publish material of such character. This evolution in structure, then, has been but a reflection of the rise of the scientific attitude, itself a product of the capitalist system, which brought with it a fuller understanding of the essence and inevitability of human reaction.

We see, then, that in literature, besides its content, the choice and arrangement of incident, the description and analysis of character, are likewise determined by environment. Now let us turn to the literature that followed Whitman, the literature of the late 90's and the twentieth century. The rise of labor organizations, a necessity for the expression of proletarian class-consciousness which was described on a previous page, was and is a constant factor in driving proletarian conceptions to the foreground. Without this rise and the impression of the proletarian upon society, novels and dramas with proletarian protagonists, treated in the serious and searching manner befitting a tragic study, would never have attained expression. This point cannot be emphasized too strongly for those idealist critics who are so prone to view the changes in literary tendencies as developments of the absolute idea or more whimsical alterations of interest and motive.

A glance at the literature of any country in which the proletariat has become a force in the social organization will reveal how very marked the literature has become by its rise. The literary artist in these lands comes to recognize that there is a soul in the common man, that the proletarian is not without his tragic affections and aspirations. And the study of these affections and aspirations becomes the subject for tragedies as elevated and sublime as those of *Œdipus* and *Athalie*. Dramas like *The Weavers, Strife,* and *Beyond the Horizon,* built about the sufferings of those of the proletariat, become masterpieces of dramatic art, and novels like *Tess of the d'Urbervilles, Frau Sorge,* and

[47]

Sons and Lovers, stories concerned with the misery and anguish of the dispossessed class, are accepted as tragedies of genuine and vital character. It should not be thought that proletarian tragedy, if such we must call it in contradistinction to the aristocratic and bourgeois, began in any particular year or with any special book, but rather that it sprang up gradually as the proletariat became more and more a class demanding social consideration. As early as 1864 in the Naturalist novel, *Germinie Lacerteux,* the Goncourts dealt with the tragic life of a servant girl,[10] and de Maupassant, although many of his stories are concerned solely with the bourgeois, gave tragic significance to the fate of Maitre Hauchecorne, the poor Norman in *A Piece of String.* These characters were treated in a different manner than was Richardson's seamstress, the difference being the consequence of the different

[10] In the preface we find an interesting and illuminating statement of the Goncourts' position: "Living in the nineteenth century, at a time of universal suffrage, and democracy, and liberalism, we asked ourselves whether what are called the 'lower orders' had no claim upon the Novel; whether the people—this world beneath a world— were to remain under the literary ban and disdain of authors who have hitherto maintained silence regarding any soul and heart that they might possess. We asked ourselves whether, in these days of equality, there were still for writer and reader unworthy classes, misfortunes that were too low, dramas too foul-mouthed, catastrophes too base in their terror. We became curious to know whether Tragedy, that conventional form of a forgotten literature and a vanished society, was finally dead; whether, in a country devoid of caste and legal aristocracy, the miseries of the lowly and the poor would speak to interest, to motion, to piety, as loudly as the miseries of the great and rich; whether, in a word, the tears that are wept below could provoke weeping like those that are wept above."

ages in which the works appeared. Hugo, of course, in many instances gave sympathetic though romantic description to the proletarian, the description, nevertheless, usually interlarded with appeals to bourgeois virtues and sentimentality. And Zola, with all of his brutality, did not fail to see and depict the strength as well as the ofttimes deep-rooted viciousness of proletarian character. All of these men, it should be noted, wrote after the revolution of 1848.

It is not until contemporary times, however, that we begin to see a steady and opulent literature growing up about the proletarian. Pierre Hamp, in France, for example, in that one collection of his stories entitled *People*, has seen great and inspiring tragedy in the life of *The Sweet Smeller* and *The Potato Sisters*. Joyce in more than one place in *Dubliners*, particularly in *The Little Cloud*, realizes the tragedy of the drab— and what is so drab as the life of the proletarian? And if we turn to American literature we meet with a very striking picture of the new concept—shall we call it the proletarian concept? Certainly it would be neither rash nor hasty criticism to say that among the most important pieces of fiction that have appeared in America during the last two decades, three works stand out very distinctly: *Ethan Frome*, by Edith Wharton; *Winesburg, Ohio*, by Sherwood Anderson, and *Sister Carrie*, by Theodore Dreiser. The protagonists in these books are proletarians and without exception the histories of their lives are woven into the texture of strange and telling tragedy. To many this fact, if it has been recognized, has not seemed to deserve notice. Yet it is of utmost significance. It mirrors the advance of the proletariat. It is additional proof that literature is the product of sociology, and can only be satisfactorily approached, studied and criticized by the sociological method.

It is because most of us today believe that the life-experience of the proletarian offers as purifying material for tragedy as that of the bourgeois or aristocrat, that we fail to realize how very brief, in historical duration, has been the existence of this attitude. The mere existence of an idea or conception too often gives the delusion of permanence.[11] What must be realized is the social process that has brought about the conditions necessary for the creation of this conception. In understanding this process, however, we do not mean to conclude that all these artists who, in their work, embody this conception are aware of the sociological factors that have made it a part of the civilization. In the greater number of instances, on the contrary, the attitude prevails, in spite of ignorance of its cause. The attitude becomes a kind of social-reflex.

---

[11] See *An Economic Approach to the Yellow Problem* by the author, which appeared in April 12th issue of *The New Leader*.

As scientific critics we cannot expect any form of society to be finally permanent, and if, as Polybius predicted, which is scarcely possible, the rise of the proletariat should be followed by an era of confusion and change, and result in the restoration of monarchy and a new system of slavery, we should discover different ethical and esthetic concepts arising to replace the proletarian. The point that must be stressed, nevertheless, is that any such change, reversion to monarchy or despotism,[12] can flow only from necessary alterations in material conditions.

Although revolutions in esthetics are due to revolutions in ideas, every revolution in ideas is a consequence of a revolution in the social structure that the prevailing material conditions have produced.

[12] These terms are used in the manner that they were applied by Montesquieu.

135729

SHERWOOD ANDERSON

A STUDY IN SOCIOLOGICAL CRITICISM

EVERY type of literature, regardless of its length or brevity of duration, or instance of appearance, has its original and motivating cause in environment. The ideas it reflects, the *genre* it cultivates, either represent, to quote Gumplowicz, the concepts of "the dominating group" or those of another group that has risen in active conflict with the dominating group, or perhaps the attenuated visions of a group that has already declined and is steadily becoming more recessive. All social changes have their corollaries in esthetics. The feudal period had its "aristocratic conception of tragedy" in perfect consonance with its social organization, its *Morte d'Arthur, King Lear,* and *Edward II;* the bourgeois ascendancy had its *London Merchant, The Gamester,* and *Sarah Simpson;* and the rising proletariat, still a subordinate but rapidly crystallizing class, has already had its *Germinie Lacerteux, The Weavers,* and *Winesburg, Ohio.* A brief study in the sociology of class-origin and development, a reference even to orthodox historians such as Madison, Guizot, and Beard, an analysis of the material conditions that foster

[52]

and perpetuate, sometimes temporarily narrowing but more often gradually widening, the different interests of these social groups, will provide abundant evidence of precisely how the clash of divergent habits of life and philosophies determine the ethical and esthetic concepts of a community.

The late Clutton-Brock, an ofttimes fascinating but haphazard critic, in an essay on art made one of his most searching and pregnant observations:

"The value of criticism consists not in the judgment, but in the process by which it is arrived at." [1]

And it is particularly in the process of criticism, the manner of approach and dissection, that the sociological method has been neglected. Impressionistic criticism, the writing of polite, poetical essays about the work of others, was cultivated long before the eighteenth century and has ripened but little in the succeeding generations. The attack upon the problem launched by Taine was revolutionary but unthorough. The appeal to *the moment* and to inherent *race-bias* was ineffectual. As Robertson keenly indicated, Taine entirely failed to see that many differences in psychology between the English and French people were purely due to their relative stages of industrial development.[2]

[1] *Essays on Art—A Defense of Criticism*—p. 51.
[2] *Buckle and His Critics*—J. M. Robertson—p. 454.

Moreover, Taine's political attitude and his lack of evolutionary outlook severely limited the finest of his work. His volume, *de l'Intelligence,* in which he constructs a kind of geometric determinism and elaborately develops the law of causality, is entitled to more praise, judged as a piece of scientific criticism, than his studies in literature. In his discussion of painting, however, especially in reference to the change of interest in the landscape, and the social causes that resulted in the rise of the landscape as an object for esthetic treatment, he came closer to the sociological approach than in any other of his criticism.[3] Buckle progressed further than Taine. Were it not for a patriotic British bias, admitted with regret by his enthusiastic devotee, J. M. Robertson, a reckless and shallow advocacy of *laissez-faire* economics, and a too zealous appeal to the effects of The Protective Spirit upon history and literature, Buckle might have developed sociological criticism further than any mind of the nineteenth century. Unfortunately, also, he did not see the essence and significance of class-conflict and its effects upon art as well as ethics. As it is, nevertheless, his work is remarkably keen and comprehensive; a notably important though incomplete contribution to sociological analysis. Earlier than either of these men, Vico, in his first *Scienza Nuova* (1725) had endeavored to subject the

[3] *Voyage aux Pyrenees.* Cinquieme edition. Paris, 1867.

substance of poetry to a somewhat scientific criticism, but his method, encumbered with vague conceptions of intellect and sensation, of the meaning of rational and spiritual, and freighted with metaphysical abstraction, did not lead him to very important general conclusions. Lessing, also a predecessor of Buckle and Taine, did not, despite his brilliant differentiation of the arts in Laokoön (1766), and his attempt to demonstrate certain laws that each must necessarily follow, advance the sociological attitude.[4] Pisarev, the Russian critic of the 60's, presents an interesting and illuminating example of what might be described as the moralizing sociological conception, although he does not perceive the evolutionary character of past esthetic concepts and the necessary trend of those that are to follow. His attitude is more didactic than scientific. George Plechanoff, the Russian materialist, elucidated the sociological method with more completeness and exactitude than any of his forerunners. He possessed wider historical perspective than the others, realized more clearly and precisely the influence and significance of the various stages of biological and historical evolution, and excluded from his inferences anything of purely speculative, patriotic or sentimental character. In his brilliant and extensive essay entitled *Art and Social*

[4] His play *Sarah Simpson* (1755) nevertheless marked a signal advance, the full importance and economic implications of which Lessing himself did not see, in the sociology of the drama in Germany.

Life, literature is subjected to rare and penetrating sociological criticism, and in parts of *Materialism and Art* painting as well as literature is given the same treatment. Plechanoff is perhaps the most thorough and piercing critic of the latter part of the nineteenth and beginning of the twentieth centuries. Sainte Beuve and J. M. Robertson have extended the biographical method and fortified it with all of the weapons of erudition at their ready and dexterous command. Mordell has developed the psychographic method which differs from the biographic chiefly in its efforts to carry its study of character to the unconscious—the cravings of the libido, in other words, the erotic motive—instead of being content with examination of the simple and deceptive manifestations of ordinary consciousness. The knowledge in this field as yet is too shadowy and uncertain for such criticism to have acquired scientific value. "It will be found that a man's work can be better understood in the light of a knowledge of his temperament and character," wrote Robertson in accurate though bromidic justification of the biographic approach, but it should be seen by all who are the least acute in their observations that knowledge of an author's "temperament and character" can be understood only in the light of his social environment. The study of temperament and character as basic coördinates in criticism, the groundwork from which to examine a piece of art, is superficial and unsatisfactory. Temperament and character are immediate, not underlying, causes. Temperament and character are effects of a more fundamental cause. The real cause to be studied is social environment, not temperament and character, which are but products of social environment, and change and intensify with every fluctuation of this environment.[5] Every social environment has its respective esthetic concepts, all in agreement with the stage of social structure, and all expressive of one group or another in its organization. No artist can escape the influence of these conceptions. In fact, these conceptions make him. In illustration we can employ Anderson's felicitous sentence: "The dust of my civilization was in my soul." [6]

In pursuing our critical study of Sherwood Anderson, therefore, we shall avoid the circumlocutory and superficial method of most of our earlier and contemporary critics, and proceed directly to those forces in the social environment that have created the very esthetic tendencies and concepts which are embodied

---

[5] If the theory of evolution be correct, heredity is but a product of environment and must inevitably change with alteration in environment. A son of a Hindu prince brought to America shortly after birth and forced to live in this country in an environment similar to that of other American bourgeois the rest of his life, will develop a series of mental reactions similar to those of the surrounding individuals, not those of his ancestors. This is so simple as to need no further amplification.

[6] *Mid-American Chants*, p. 26.

in the work of the author under discussion. Our
analysis shall be historical and yet immediate. To
trace not only the influence but the undeviating course
of these social changes in affecting literature, particularly the fiction and poetry of Mr. Anderson, shall be
the paramount purpose of our task. From the criticism
that we shall project, it should be clear at the conclusion that every artist is fettered by the conceptions of
his age, that his work cannot be successfully studied
as a detached phenomenon, and that the nature of these
conceptions which determine the nature of the art
are the result of distinct class-conflicting sociological
factors.

2

With reasonable precision, we can divide the late developments of capitalism, since the conclusion of the
Civil War, into three periods. The first period, extending until 1875, marked the rise of large industry; the
second period, continuing until 1890 at least, saw the
evolution of "great industry"; and the third period,
still in the process of active concentration, reveals the
steady centralization of industry into gigantic corporations and monopolies.[7] From these various changes in

[7] So far these corporations and monopolies are largely nationalistic
in organization, but with the growing interdependence of the whole
of capitalism upon its countless parts, they will inevitably expand
and assume an international character. With this change, of course—
and it is gradually occurring at the present moment—will come a

industrial structure have flowed corresponding changes in class-organization. With the disappearance of free lands in the west, which for a time were an intruding factor, the proletariat has necessarily increased as wealth has concentrated, and its method of struggle, if not objective, has altered with the entrance of new economic factors. Until its rise as a class-unit it could have no effect on social consciousness and in no way create any enduring esthetic concepts. Literary concepts included nothing of the proletariat during the feudal period (*cf.* aristocratic conception of tragedy), or during the early history of the supremacy of the bourgeois; only when the proletariat by its very organization and intensification, its awakening into a real class-consciousness, made itself felt as a vigorous part of the social body, did a literature begin to spring up about it and esthetic concepts take its existence into consideration. During the feudal period, for instance, the opportunity for a proletarian to become an author was comparatively small, and even if he did achieve such success *we never find him endeavoring to*

---

desire for peace throughout that part of the world which will be knit into an economic whole, and also, due to the rise of the revolutionary tendency in the labor movement, will follow a more strenuous clamor and demand for a new system of distribution. From these fluctuating economic conditions, already there have arisen hosts of Christian and pagan pacifists, reckless advocates of Leagues of Nations and world courts, although the material factors are certainly not ripe enough for the disappearance of American Legions and Citizens' Training Camps.

*change the existing esthetic attitude or trying to intro-
duce the proletariat as fit material for tragedy.* In
simple terms, then, we do not find the proletariat dealt
with as appropriate substance for tragedy, the highest
form of literature and about which have revolved these
various concepts, until it has grown into a significant
and undeniable class-unit. We do not discover *Germinie Lacerteuxs* during the sixteenth century, *Isaac
Sheftels* during the seventeenth, or *Winesburg, Ohios,*
during the eighteenth or first half of the nineteenth
century. A group of stories such as *Winesburg, Ohio,*
or a novel such as *Marching Men* could not have appeared before the revolution of 1848. The proletarian
was quite clearly described in the dispute between
Madison and Pinckney at the time of the Constitutional Convention.

Sherwood Anderson's work, therefore, as we shall
see more vividly with further dissection, affords an
excellent introduction to what we may call the proletarian concept exemplified in literature. During the
feudal period and throughout the early part of the
bourgeois ascendency, until the middle of the last century, the "common man" was not believed to possess
the "soul" that such authors as Whitman, Norris, Anderson, Hamp, Dreiser, Pinski, Hardy and others have
seen in him. The point that must be stressed, however,
is that this new attitude, this new vision of the life and

nature of the working man, are not the result of any sudden and spontaneous determination on the part of artists to appreciate the indescribable tragedy of his existence, but the consequence of changing social conditions which have made such determination, such interest, possible. Without the industrial evolution of the nineteenth century and the organization of the proletariat, such *determination,* such *interest,* would have been impossible.

*　　*　　*　　*　　*　　*　　*　　*

In criticism of a work of art we should establish our coördinates in the beginning and be careful to keep them constantly in mind when making a judgment. In the criticism of a story great meticulousness of selection is needed. There is not only the purpose and proposition that the author had in mind which we must consider, but also the nature of our own mental and emotional reactions that are evoked by the reading. Where possible, the state of the mind of the critic antecedent to the reading-experience should be noted and weighed before deriving a conclusion. In criticizing a story we can state the following propositions in explanation of how we have come to our judgments; in doing this work we are fully cognizant of the necessary looseness and vagueness of the coördinates, a characteristic that we cannot avoid in the present chaos of human impulse and predilection, a chaos that will be obliterated only with an increasing equality and comparative uniformity of environment.

To be significant, a story, unless it be a mere romance, must possess:

(a) Exactitude of representation, aided by carefulness and opulence of selection.

(b) Uniqueness of theme, without the unconvincing elements of the "unique thriller."

(c) Inevitability of action—"characters must perform only those actions which, in the nature of their being, it was impossible for them not to perform"—which naturally flows from requirement (a), and yet it is necessary to emphasize it.

(d) Descriptions in keeping with the theme, not over-long or over-detailed, devoted to creating a verbal, not a pictorial art.

(e) Elegance of structure—a story, after all, is a form of art, of artifice if you will, and is not and cannot be a reality itself. It is foolish for art to aspire to such purpose. There must be an arrangement of incident and character so as to get the best artistic effect.

1. Events should lead to a climax.
2. The concatenation of description and episode should arouse suspense, or if the story is told in a straightforward style these elements should invite interest by the pure appeal of the immediate setting.

(f) There should be a well-defined philosophy of life embodied in the style and substance—this

[62]

should not reveal itself in didactic form, but in the whole manner of approach and study of the characters and their relations to their environment.

(g) The reader must come from the story emotionally if not intellectually stimulated. A story does not claim to advance scientific thought, clearly outline a system of philosophy, or develop a scheme of psychology. On the other hand, it does offer a medium for larger experience, and it is the craving for more varied and intense experience than the usualness of things affords that drives most readers to fiction as a means of a vicarious fulfillment of their desires. In this sense, if in no other, a story functions as a means of satisfying the human desire for projection, as well as awakening profound emotional reaction. In all events, if a story be great, it must move us while reading, impress us with its substance, and leave us with an emotion that is vivid and unforgettable. Without this effect the story may be interesting, entertaining, charming to peruse, but certainly not *great*.

We do not mean to conclude from this that every story of value must embody all of these elements, though the finest stories necessarily will, but that they are the criteria which we set up as a sound basis for criticism of such material. [8] At least they are clarify-

[8] We cannot enter here into a discussion of the influence of the method of Cezanne upon modern fiction, or point out its limitations and philosophic fallacy.

ing as to attitude and serve as an approach to more definiteness in the matter of interpretation and judgment.

*   *   *   *   *   *   *   *

During the 70's, when Sherwood Anderson was born, the Midwest was just beginning to emerge from the slow quietude of an agricultural age. The small towns that Anderson knew as a boy changed greatly in the years of his youth and early manhood. Villages sprang into towns and towns into cities almost in the mad swiftness of a night—"like a great flood over it all the coming of the factories, the coming of modern industrialism.[9] The "slow culture" in the villages and towns "that had been growing up through the hands of workmen" was shattered by the invasion of machinery with its hastening mass and concentration of production. Hamlets once barren and desolate, at the discovery of oil in the vicinity, sprang into violent unnatural life. The population of the west began to multiply. With the increase and crowding together of the people came the social changes that always follow such a vicissitude.

"In all of the towns and over the wide countryside of my own Mid-American boyhood there was no such thing as poverty, as I myself saw it and knew it later in our great American industrial towns and cities."[10]

[9] *A Story Teller's Story,* Sherwood Anderson's autobiography. Part I, Note 1.
[10] *Ibid.*

With the disappearance of the listless, leisurely, un-progressive atmosphere of the small towns, the spread of population and poverty, a new psychology received its birth. "Solid respectable men, with money in the bank" made the investments, promoted the shooting of wells and the erection of factories, and divided the spoils. The Aldrichs and McPhersons became more numerous and more oppressed. A distinct line of demarcation began to pencil itself between the men who "walked about smoking twenty-five cent cigars," creating Lima booms and plotting and counterplotting against the failure or usurpation of their enterprise, and the penniless toiling farmers and mechanics of The New Age. Their interests quickly and sharply separated, although the latter were slow to realize it. This under-standing of their social situation was not to come until the economic system had intensified and severely sub-jected them to its irresistible pressure.

Labor unions had begun to organize in the East early in the nineteenth century, and though they were able to effect certain minor reforms, it was not until after 1850 that they received legal recognition. In many cases before the middle of the century men were pun-ished for trying to organize themselves for the purpose of strike and other maneuvers of collective bargaining. In one instance the verdict reads:

"We find the defendants guilty of a combination to raise their wages. The defendants were each fined eight dollars with costs of the suit and (were) committed until paid."[11]

The proletariat does not organize if it is content with its situation. Such organization in the beginning proceeds from discontent, and, unless an intelligent class-consciousness has been created, weakens with periods of exceptional freedom and prosperity. The development of anti-union societies, fostered by employers, during the late sixties and seventies, sharpened the issue. The plan for an industrial congress of capitalists, designed for the purpose of regulating wages and hours throughout the country and combatting union labor, hastened the temporary unification of the proletariat. The encouragement of Oriental immigration aggravated the animosity still further.[12] The labor press was revived.[13] There was a resolution that a National Labor Party be organized in 1868, and

[11] *A Documentary History of American Industrial Society,* Vol. III; and Oneal's *Workers in American History.*

[12] The conference of planters and capitalists that met in Memphis, July, 1869, made use of the most singular and amusing rationalization that history has to record: "China especially is capable of supplying us with a class of laborers peculiarly adapted to our circumstances," the report of the conference said, and added as a triumph, "whilst we avail ourselves of the physical assistance these pagans are capable of affording us, (we) endeavor at the same time to bring to bear upon them the elevating and saving influence of our holy religion."

[13] Fincher's *Trade Review* was started June, 1863, and between the years 1863 and 1873 over 120 labor periodicals were started.

in the next year "a labor party in Massachusetts elected representatives to the Legislature and one State Senator." A. C. Cameron, one of the leaders of this labor movement, a delegate to Basle Congress, declared in 1867:

"There is but one dividing line, that which separates mankind into two great classes, the class that labors and the class that lives by others' labors."[14]

This is a clear-cut expression of the attitude of at least a segment of the proletariat at the time. The Knights of Labor, organized by Uriah Stephens in 1869, became an open and significant element in the struggle only after 1881. In 1886 it had a membership of over seven hundred thousand. The Socialist Labor Party had come into existence in 1877 and made its first national campaign in 1892, the same year that saw the birth and rise of the People's Party. The Haymarket episode, May 4, 1886, of course, hindered the progress of the proletariat for a considerable period. Since that time numerous developments have taken place. The split in the Socialist Labor Party in 1899, the organization of the ephemeral Socialist Democratic Party in 1901, the beginning of the Socialist Party, the coming of the Industrial Workers of the World, and finally, after the last war, the organization of the

[14] *Documentary History,* Vol. I. Pages 158, 159.

Workers' Party, a hasty sprout of the Bolshevik Party in Russia, are but a few of the salient events to be noted.

All of this political history has been described because it gives a vivid picturesque sketch of the growth and organization of the proletariat in the United States, which is essential to an understanding of how the proletariat has been able to influence and change the prevailing ethical and esthetic conceptions of earlier centuries. The attitudes of philosophers and artists in society, we reiterate, are but a reflection, a rationalization it may even be termed, of the social structure, of the ideas of some one group or another, sometimes an unfelicitous neutralization of the ideas of several groups, that constitute the scaffolding of this structure. A group, or class, it is necessary to state again, will make little impression upon social consciousness, upon the concepts which society has established, if it lacks definiteness of purpose and form. Sporadic strikes of masons in Egypt (about 1000 B. C.), of musicians in Rome (309 B. C.), secret labor organizations advocating sentimental economics, are not sufficient cause to bring about a change in the reigning conceptions. Only with the intense centralization of capitalism, with all of the social concomitants that necessarily follow in the train of such a phenomenon, could a well-defined proletarian class-consciousness develop and magnify.

Not before this social change, then, could anything like a *proletarian* concept flourish, or could artists give the proletarian the tender and meditative consideration, from an esthetic point of view, that he now receives.

Sherwood Anderson's works are a product of this social trend. The difference between his attitude toward the proletarian and that of Goldsmith, himself a born proletarian, or that of Samuel Johnson or Pope, can be conclusively traced to precisely the social changes we have described, the rise of the proletariat as a result of the industrial oppression and concentration of capitalism. The proletarian becomes as fit subject for tragedy as the son of a king or merchant. Anderson has discovered powerful tragedy in the lives of these common people, tragedy as pervasive and poignant as any to be found in the classic drama of previous periods. Anderson is a child of this environment. He knew the towns when "the tired berry pickers walked home from the fields in the dust of the roads swinging their dinner pails," and the "old men lit their pipes and sat gossiping along the curbing at the edge of the sidewalk on Main Street," when "the people . . . were to each other like members of a great family"; and then he saw these towns go through their cyclonic change, saw "the new force that was being born into American life . . . the new force (that) stirred and aroused people, (that) was meant to seal men together, to wipe out national lines, to walk under seas and fly through the air, to change the entire face of the world in which men lived." To Sherwood Anderson, therefore, this new order was no abstraction. His description of its coming is a living description of his own personal impressions, his own life.

Sherwood Anderson could no more have devoted his art to the construction of aristocratic or bourgeois tragedy than Shakespeare could have been a propagandist for democracy. Anderson is the avatar of the proletarian movement. From his work arise the subtle exhalation of the fields at sundown when men are toiling at their crops and women slaving before their fires, and the blackened streams of smoke that spout from factory roofs where men work day after day for wives and offspring starving in the squalid quarters of rushing, turbulent cities. His words ring with the cry of the proletarian. They are resonant with protest and indignation. They are mad with the despair and ennui of a dying civilization.

3

Anderson's first novel to appear, *Windy McPherson's Son,* is dedicated to

> *the living men and women*
> *of my own middle western home town,*

and *Marching Men,* his second production, to

American Workingmen;

neither to Lord Chesterfield, nor His Highness the Duke of Schnitzenberg. This is significant as a revelation of the distinct change of social attitude that we have described in our preceding analysis. According to Mr. Hansen, a personal friend of Mr. Anderson, *Marching Men* had been in large part if not entirely finished at the time that *Windy McPherson's Son* appeared in 1916, and it is not altogether improbable that both novels were written, in the fashion of Dostoievsky, at approximately the same period. Both books are unquestionably immature efforts, suffering from the divagations of a groping but unoriented artist. They have a continuity of purpose but not of structure. Their realism, springing from the atmosphere of the town and later of the city, is without the sapidity of life, a kind of blundering, suspended realism, even and drab in parts and wildly melodramatic in others, escaping romanticism only by their vividness of setting.

Windy McPherson's Son, with all of its satire and revolt, belongs to the *great man* period of Anderson's development. The protagonists in both of his early novels fall into this category. Sam McPherson and Beaut McGregor are not men of common clay, but individuals endowed with marvelous acuteness and energy, inflexibly purposed, born to create and command. There is nothing of the tender simplicity and withdrawing gesture of Wing Biddlebaum about them, nothing of the indolence, ordinariness, or incapacity. They belong to the youth of capitalism when "one went into a factory, did his work with care and skill, became foreman, superintendent, part owner, married the banker's daughter, got rich and perhaps went off to Paris to sin the sins neglected during so busy a youth and early manhood," [15]—or when one could have done those things, when the opportunity was not already foreclosed. Despite the promise of the changed Sam McPherson that "he would try to spend his life seeking truth" and that of McGregor that he would bring into being his visionary conception of *Marching Men,* one perceives an echo of the Nietzschean warcry about their very words and actions. This tendency to create "great men," this form of vicarious heroworship, disappears with pleasant swiftness in Anderson's latest novels and stories.

Sam McPherson is the embodiment of the philosophy of the discontented capitalist. Inspired by the counsel of John Tilfer, the artist who has receded into the obscurity of the small town, and who has devoted his later life to the "art of living" instead of the "art of painting," Sam at an early age set himself to the task

[15] *A Story Teller's Story,* Sherwood Anderson, Part I, Note IV.

of "money-making," determined to let neither procrastination nor sentiment swerve him from his purpose. The youth's success is incredibly phenomenal. The situations that favor him flow with too ingratiating an ease to have about them the element necessary to realistic art: inevitability. The simple, almost Alger-like dovetailing of incidents fails to conjure up the illusion of reality—and it is the vividness of that illusion that is the criterion of realistic art.

Let us make our analysis more specific and complete. Anderson, like Scott, is always better when he deals with his original environment. Just as Scott did his best work in *The Heart of Midlothian* and *Old Mortality*, novels laid in the heart of his homeland and devoted to a description of his native people, Anderson has done his best work in his stories and novels, or at least those parts of his novels, that are laid in the small town, and devoted to a description of the characteristics of its curious sex-repressed folk. Had *Windy McPherson's Son* ended at the conclusion of Book I, the work could have been accused of incompleteness, but not of lack of cogency. The moment that Sam McPherson is withdrawn from the surroundings of Caxton, Iowa, his adventures become high-flown and unconvincing. In the corn-shipping town of Caxton, Sam McPherson, John Tilfer, Mike McCarthy, and drunken Windy are characters palpitating with life, performing tangible, natural acts, expressing atittudes thoroughly consistent with their heritage and environment. One can understand the silent defiance of Mary Underwood, admire the uncanny placidity of temperament of Jane McPherson, laugh at old Freedom's passion for "buying up half-worn buggies and agricultural implements," and not once doubt the clear reality of their actions. While Sam's attempted murder of his father, an excited, flaming event, does not flavor of melodrama—melodrama being defined as that type of literature in which action and not character-sequence is made paramount—his early strides in business most certainly and dismally do. That the medical student, Eckardt, should consent to let Sam McPherson have his fortune of $20,000 to invest, without holding the latter the least responsible even if the money were lost, or requiring that he pay more than seven per cent interest if it reaped dividends, is ridiculously absurd and unnatural. The episode is further made to lack the persuasiveness of reality by Sam's admission to himself that "the kind of deals that he expected to make with the money . . . would frighten and alarm (Eckardt)." Yet the improbable is achieved with a smoothness more utopian than real. Again in the episode with Luella London, the actress, the same stunt is duplicated. That an actress so sophisticated as the coquettish Luella should risk her newly acquired

$10,000 in the care of Sam, the very man who not fifteen minutes before had deceived her by his cunning, is even more difficult to swallow. Later, the attitude of the *changed* Sam is more convincing in the light of his *old* nature than are the bewildering series of events into which he is so haphazardly plunged. The structure of the last part of the novel, Books III and IV, is grotesquely unsymmetrical. That a man of the aggressive personality of Sam McPherson when passionately bent upon "the search of truth," should perform the race of unconnected acts that he does in his wild roaming across country is hard to reconcile with our previous knowledge of his character. The finale particularly is weak and unsuccessful. We can easily detect about it that quality of falseness which we instantaneously notice in a forced rhyme, for instance, or a discordant note. That a woman such as Belle should be willing to surrender her children to a stranger we can imagine, but that Sam should seize them with such avidity and then dash back to Sue, the wife who had deserted him and with whom he had so little commonness of affection, is an impingement upon our gullibility. And further—that Sue, because of her crying desire for maternity which had motivated her marriage with Sam, should accept with complaisance his return with three children of another woman, is a solution, an ending, quite forced and esthetically unfelicitous.

In conclusion of our discussion of his novel, it is well for us to repeat that in the small town, among its sloping valleys and waving hills, its drowsy superstitious populace, Anderson is perfect master of his material; removed from it his material too often seems to master him.

In *Marching Men* we meet with many of the same characteristics that we discovered in *Windy McPherson's Son*. The style in both novels is rough and amorphous, without the rhythmical succession of phrase, the simple and eloquent imagery, that we find in the best passages of *Winesburg, Ohio, Poor White,* and *Many Marriages*. Instances of the unpolished nature of the style are discouragingly abundant. If, for instance, we take the death of Nance McGregor, the mother of Beaut, we can readily see the inferiority of Anderson's earlier style to that which is acquired with the later maturing of his talent:

"Nance sat stiffly up in bed. She thought she heard the sound of heavy feet on the stairs. 'That will be Beaut coming up from the shop,' she muttered and fell back upon the pillow dead."[16]

This is scarcely an exaggeration of the impoverished style that runs through the whole novel. The parts given to dialogue are not superior in force or diction.

[16] *Marching Men,* page 136.

The speech is stilted, entirely minus that ringing clarity of utterance which vivifies the words of May Edgely or John Webster. As in the previous novel, the first one hundred pages, over a half of which are concerned with the life of the McGregors in the town of Coal Creek, Pennsylvania, contain more vigorous and successful narration than the remaining two hundred.

The characterization, however, is neither so fine nor so penetrating as in parts of *Windy McPherson's Son.* Cracked McGregor, the courageous miner, mentally unbalanced as a result of an accident in the mine, stolid, taciturn and defiant as an Indian, is a figure that emerges clearly from the dull, murky background of the early part of the novel; likewise Beaut McGregor, the protagonist, an aggressive pugnacious personality, an inexorable votary of orderliness, stands out with singular strength and luminousness, first in the thickened atmosphere of Coal Creek and later in the legal and labor vortices of Chicago.

Although both of these characters are distinct, clearcut individualities, as haunting as many of the caricatures of Dickens, they have about them the trappings more of romantic than realistic portraiture. Their lineaments are clear, their actions sharply scissored from the setting, yet, in many ways, they are very unreal. This, at first glance, seems paradoxical. But it is not. A griffin or a gargoyle can be painted with the vividness of great art, yet in the sense that it represents *nothing real* in life it cannot be called *realistic;* a giant may be so described in a fairy tale that he seems to live with a tenseness more moving than that of a Rosalind Westcott or a Melville Stoner, but his size and the things he does are so incongruous with our knowledge of life, that, however fascinating, we could not legitimately classify him as a type of realistic art. The griffin may be a rare piece of romantic painting, an exquisite grotesque, a soaring exemplification of the extent of human fantasy, but criticism of it must be strictly confined within the circles of romanticism. As a form of realism, despite the brilliance and symmetry of its separate segments, it has no value. So it is with *certain* of Anderson's characters, they are enormous and distinct as giants, titanic conceptions, gesturing like gods, veritable masters of circumstance—impressive but unreal. Realistic art is founded upon the principle of resemblance, that esthetic pleasure is derived from exactitude of representation, heightened by the power of selection. The introduction of elements that are without the likelihood of reality depreciates the realism into something tawdry and ineffective. Romantic-realism is a bastard *genre.* If an artist intends a piece of realism, his substance must be pure of allegory and magic, of anything that is not an inevitable consequent of its antecedents.

[78]

In the case of *Windy McPherson's Son,* we indicated its fallacies from the point of view of a consistent realism, and we shall now do the same with *Marching Men.* Although the urbanized Sam McPherson should be classified among the Andersonian characters of romantic proportions, he belongs not so essentially to that category as do Beaut McGregor and David Ormsby, both salient characters in *Marching Men.* Beaut McGregor is one of those giants that we described above, giants that interest and impress us with the largeness of their stature but not with the reality of their action. The Beaut McGregor of Chicago is a portentous magnification of the Beaut McGregor of Coal Creek, Pennsylvania. In Coal Creek there are no strange or distorted circumstances to disturb our belief in his conduct; in Chicago there are a host of such. In Coal Creek he is an impetuous, sex-groping youth, another Sam McPherson made defiant by a maelstrom of town-hostilities; in Chicago he is a common laborer, rising through the fortuitous help of a girl to the position of lawyer, and later through a miracle of circumstances acquiring an "over-night" reputation as a criminal attorney. There is a noticeable sentimentality of description in this advance of McGregor from the position of menial to that of master. This, however, might be overlooked were it not for the romantic developments that proceed from this source.

Beaut McGregor is harassed by the unsightly chaos of human thought and activity, the wild clash of individual impulse and purpose. He is obsessed with a desire for *orderliness*, for design amid this confusion. This craving becomes a mania, demanding active not contemplative expression. Sheer intellectual speculation, dreamful theorizing in historical abstraction, are an abomination to one of his temperament. He is in vital revolt against the cabinet-retreat of the student and philosopher. His life is a cry for vigorous *organized* force, perpetually in motion, ceaselessly advancing, defiant and invincible.

As a symphony of impulse, a drama of the grandiose, *Marching Men* is a moving and picturesque novel; as a piece of realism, which it purports to be, it fails of solidity and conviction. We marvel at the eloquent McGregor heading his countless ranks of marching men. He is imperious and inexorable, inspired with the faith of a fanatic in the efficacy of his ideal. In our enthusiasm, for a moment, we almost come to believe in him, to accept the situation as a reality of the esthetic. Removed from the immediacy of the object, however, our emotions more tranquillized, we are forced to change our judgment. He is *another giant,* an apotheosis of an ideal rather than the crystallization of an idea, a personification of a movement, not an individuality. His achievements are illogical—melodramatic. They belong to another civilization than ours, a civilization constructed upon a different ethic. Men could not have been made to march in the fashion of McGregor's squads if they were employed and lived at the time and under the social conditions in which they were placed. There is something exceedingly romantic about the drilling and chanting of these proletarian groups, marching unarmed in endless procession in town and city over all the country.

"And then the movement of the Marching Men began to come to the surface. It got into the blood of men. That harsh drumming voice began to shake their hearts and legs.

"Everywhere men began to see and hear of the Marchers. From lip to lip ran the question, 'What's going on?'

" 'What's going on?' How that cry ran over Chicago. Every newspaper man in town got assignments on the story. The papers were loaded with it every day. All over the city they appeared, everywhere,—the Marching Men. . . .

"Of course the police tried to stop the marchers. Into a street they would run crying 'Disperse!' The men did disperse only to appear again on some vacant lot working away at the perfection of the marching. Only an excited squad of police captured a company of them. The same men were back in line the next evening. The police could not arrest a hundred thousand men because they marched shoulder to shoulder along the streets and chanted a weird march song as they went."

To anyone the least acquainted with our social system such description is palpably absurd. Our recent experience has proved that without chance of doubt. If the police could not arrest these chanting hordes, and the very sentence implies that such was (and had to be) the wish and object of the upper class, the militia would have been summoned to conclude the demonstrations. A dozen pretexts could have been invented. *Agent-provocateurs* could have been employed, as may have been the case in the Haymarket riot of '86, if no other means could have been devised. Further, the disalliance of the movement with any political or economic policy or any method of definite reform taxes our credulity beyond endurance. Men do not march for the rhythm of marching, nor involve themselves in movements without knowledge of their purpose and finality—nor without promise of reward!

> "We do not think and banter words.
> We march."

These two verses of their song express their movement. There is no clean, steady plan that directs their enthusiasm, no *orderliness* of design, except the *orderliness* of marching. "We will not talk or listen to talk —but march . . . on and on forever." This is roman-

[82]

tic psychology and sociology—it is not fidelity to reality.

David Ormsby, "the quiet efficient representative of wealth," is an exaggerated type of antithesis. His psychology, an embodiment of the attitude of the capitalist, is softened by a strange and grasping affection for his daughter Margaret who, despite her vacillation of sentiment, is in love with McGregor. He is a colorless abstraction, anemic and pulseless. His opposition to McGregor, pallid and feeble though it is, is easily comprehensible, but his attempt to discourage his daughter's admiration for the leader of the Marching Men and convert her to his philosophy, his platitudinizing explanations and defense, are the actions of a puppet, done without vigor or vitality. He is another giant, less winning and magnetic, however, than the stalwart, flaming McGregor.

Nevertheless, with all of its inconsistencies of character and situation, *Marching Men* possesses unique significance in American literature. It is radiantly and romantically symbolic of the rise of the proletariat. The tragic cry of the workingman finds passionate echo in the voice of McGregor.

"I am going to fight the comfortable well-to-do acceptance of a disorderly world, the smug men who see nothing wrong in a world like this. I would like to fight them so that they throw their cigars away and run about like ants when you kick over ant-hills in the fields."[17]

The effect of the organization of the proletariat, a result of industrial limitation and oppression, obtains vivid and unmistakable reflection in this curious novel. The decay of an old and the synthesis of a new civilization are implicit in the substance of the narrative. An apprehension of class-conflict, a sociological element that must insistently permeate modern art, also is to be noticed in the startling chapters at the close of the story. The laboring man is seen to have a *soul*. His life, the author realizes, is rich with material of tragedy, tragedy as poignant and powerful certainly as that of the classical past. In reflecting this esthetic attitude, Anderson deserves particular notice as embodying the new and advanced concept of the rising group in society.

4

If we should apply the criterion of Count Caylus that the test of a poet, or the means of determining his rank—and we could subsume fiction under Caylus' classification—is the number of paintings that his work offers the artist, or the excellency of material presented for this purpose, we could consider *Marching Men* superior to *Winesburg, Ohio*. Of course, we have come

[17] *Marching Men.*

[84]

to agree with Lessing in entirety that a poetical (or fictional) painting "need not of necessity be convertible into a material one," and also to realize that the psychographic details of modern fiction make its descriptions clearly untransmutable into any other form of art. *Winesburg, Ohio,* for instance, which represents the peak of Anderson's achievements, is a finished piece of word-imagery devoted to the elucidation of the psychology of small-town life. The collection of stories of which it is constituted, all revolving about the characters of a single town, is replete with details of mental experience that could be presented upon no other canvas than a verbal. The stories are completely clear of the tortured juggling of melodrama. They are psychic studies, attaining physical action only when necessary to complement the mental background. They represent the *proletarian* concept with finer clarity and precision than any other stories or novels that have appeared in America during this generation.

Here we find the plain characters of life, the ignorant toilers of the fields, the obscure doctor, the simple preacher, all described with sympathetic and penetrating insight. There is no didacticism to mar the pristine beauty of style and substance. No *great man* element is introduced as in *Windy McPherson's Son* and *Marching Men* to disturb the harmony of the realism. There are no giants or gigantesques, no romantic heroes or heroines, nothing but clearly chiseled personalities, instinct with the cravings and aspirations of life. Wing Biddlebaum is one of those quaint inverted personalities that walk unobtrusively through the streets of towns and cities in every part of the world. His hands, "the piston rods of his machinery of expression," are symbolic of the touching tragedy of his warm and affectionate nature. His failure is described with a rare and unaffected simplicity. There is none of the ranting of the ebullient Lesbian about his attitude or speech, nothing of the darkened decadence of a Wilde or Verlaine. One does not hear this Biddlebaum compare himself with Jesus or Michael Angelo, or justify his twisted desires in ecstatic and intoxicated poetics. He is blind to all these things. He is a plain man, loving to teach because of the closeness of contact with boys which this profession affords. Wing Biddlebaum did not, or should I say in justice to his creator, does not, understand himself. It is that attitude which furnishes the profound and moving psychology of his life. This character is unforgettable. In writing of Wing Biddlebaum we recall at once that statement of Anderson's that a character delineated by an author "often is more living than the living one from whom it came." Wash Williams, the hideous telegraph-operator of Winesburg, with his seeming beastliness of habits and motive, his filthy garments and drunken gymnastics, his violent misogynism, is no less convincing and vital a character than the protagonist in *Hands*. Here is a trace of sublimity, a tender pathos, in the tragic career of this proletarian:

"Not everything about Wash was unclean. He took care of his hands. His fingers were fat, but there was something sensitive and shapely in the hands that lay on the table by the instrument in the telegraph office."

This recalls to us that memorable passage in *A Story Teller's Story* where Anderson confesses his admiration for the labor of the workingman:

"A slow culture growing up, however—growing as culture must always grow—through the hands of workmen.

"In the small towns artisans coming in—the harness maker, the carriage builder, the builder of wagons, the smith, the tailor, the maker of shoes, the builder of houses and barns, too.

"As Slade and James were to be fathers of the modern gunmen, so these, the fathers of the artists of the generations to come. In their fingers the beginning of that love of surface, of the sensual love of materials, without which no true civilization can ever be born."[18]

It is in the introduction of a single unique situation in the form of a climax but more often in the very

[18] *A Story Teller's Story*, page 142. Phantasmus, Vol. I, No. 2.

heart of the narrative, that saves many of Anderson's stories from the taint of *ordinariness*. In *Respectability*, for instance, despite the singular appeal of Wash Williams, it is the unexpected entrance of the wife, nude and ashamed—the wife to whom Williams thought he might return—that sets off the story as strange and forceful. In *Godliness*, to take another example, the idea of sacrifice that obsesses the demented religious mind of Jesse Bentley establishes the story in the memory with an indelible impressiveness.

These stories have a flawless rhythm and a quality of the inevitable which are unequaled in anything else that Anderson has written. Situations arise and develop without the rupture of artificiality or the crude superfœtations of the episodic "thriller." There is nothing forced about their structure and content. They have a unity that is enchanting and *natural*. The tragedy of the lives of the inhabitants of Winesburg does not have the funereal, scrannel echo of the restless spirits of Spoon River. The flare of satire and the whip of irony, devices of the subordinate literati, are absent from the delineation. Anderson's treatment of the people of Winesburg is that of a profound psychologist and a profound artist. The treatment is a distinct reflection of the growing scientific attitude of our time —the latter a result of the sociological factors we have previously described. With the progress of science and consequent inculcation of scientific theory, the attitude of an artist toward his characters, as that of a criminologist toward his criminals, has undergone marked severity of change. The extension of the law of cause and effect into sociology has resulted in revelations of astounding and revolutionary character. The inevitability of human-reaction has become increasingly apparent, in fact irrefutable. That "men's actions are the outcome of their antecedents and environment," as an English critic aptly put it, is a fact that can no longer be denied. Such a conception necessarily brings about a broad change in judgment and interpretation of action. In the literature of previous centuries and in much of today, that which is produced by artists unresponsive to the intellectual advance of their age, actions of wicked character were performed by villains and those of righteous character by heroes and heroines. The villains—except in stories of the picaresque—were uniformly and unmitigatedly condemned, while the heroes and heroines were consistently eulogized. "The passion for moralizing" was quixotically violent.[19] Characters were held responsible for their acts, regardless of their "antecedents or environment." The natu-

[19] It is interesting to note in this reference a sentence of J. M. Robertson: "The passion for moralizing a character, however, is not quite so strong today as it was in Carlyle's time, being in part superseded by the desire to understand it." That this change is due to the scientific proof of determinism, a consequence of the evolution of science, and the gradual disappearance of voluntarism with its moralizing equipment, Mr. Robertson fails to indicate.

ralists revolted from such an attitude out of pure desire to see the object clearly and avoid didacticism, and such novelists as George Eliot—influenced by the German materialism of Feuerbach—and later Thomas Hardy and Joseph Conrad expressed the same vigorous opposition. With the spread of this attitude the villain and hero, as they were formerly described, became somewhat obsolete. Bad actions were described not to inspire hatred for the actors, but as facts of life to be recognized and understood. Heroes were no longer painted as embodiments of allegorical purity, to be glassed in and stared at by the wondering and admiring eyes of peccant spectators. The change was gradual but certain.

The day of the one-sided character is past—except in the perfumed fiction of the hotel lobby and the boudoir. Mr. Anderson, of course, in his later works especially, is entirely innocent of any such gross onesidedness. The fact is he has gone further than many of the best fictionists in ethological analysis. A brief contrast here between the works of Sinclair Lewis and Sherwood Anderson will be illuminating and extremely to the point. Lewis limns the inhabitants of the small town, in *Main Street,* for instance, with an eye to their pettiness and incompetencies, derisively satirizing their handfuls of wisdom and pretenses to progress and felicity, his tongue in his cheek and his lips curled into a demonic smile. Anderson treats these small-townites in the manner of a grave and sympathetic physician— a social physician! He does not laugh at their foibles or sneer at their short-sightedness of judgment, their religiosity, pruriency, and provincialism. There is no mockery, no sarcasm, no facetiousness even, in the Anderson method. The personality struggle of a Kate Swift, in Anderson's hands, becomes a part of a universal struggle of the world. Characters are created that have flesh and blood, characters that we can visualize, feel and understand, real human beings, not troglodytes or centaurs. Their sins spring from their environment, not from any ineradicable wickedness of human nature. They err because they are driven by the implacable convergence of circumstance. Condemnation is futile. It is not for us to deprecate, but to understand. Satire in such a situation is but a vaporous evasion of the issue. "To make you hear, to make you feel—before all to make you see," which was the aim of Conrad is also the aim of Anderson as it is the aim of every genuine and great artist. It is this aim, more successfully achieved, as is to be expected, in some of his stories than others, that is implicit in everything that Anderson has written. Anderson's attitude, then, as a consequence, is that of the condoning artist, the knower of causes, the critic of conditions, the estimator of life-impulse and its origins.

This attitude, as we have shown, is an accurate reflection of the advance in science due to the advance in social evolution. There is no discontinuity in this attitude between the work of Loeb and Ferri, both scientists, and that of Hardy and Anderson, both artists; the expression of it is different, the one dispassionate and unvibrating, the other emotional and ecstatic, but in fundament they are the same. Anderson here is representing what will be the established esthetic attitude of tomorrow.

5

The other works of Sherwood Anderson proceed in line with *Winesburg, Ohio,* each projecting its own *motif* and each aspiring towards the same aim, differently colorful naturally according to the difference in content, but in no instance do they attain the same unity and excellence of utterance. *The Triumph of the Egg,* however, the collection of stories that followed *Winesburg, Ohio,* is not far behind its predecessor in value. The stories in the later volume, nevertheless, lack the connectedness of theme and character, the lucidity and concision of narrative, the vigorous and compelling simplicity, that characterize the Winesburg collection. *I Want To Know Why* is a fairly interesting tale of youth and the race track, combining a certain glimpse into adolescence with a description of the breezy swiftness and beauty of the equine form. The story, lazy in motion, weak in construction and unparsimoniously conceived, is redeemed largely by a unique and effective climax. Certainly it does not possess the revealing insight and power of such stories as *Queer* and *The Teacher*. The atmosphere, in keeping with the situation, is racy but evanescent. It suffers from formlessness and a too genial superficiality. *The Egg*, on the other hand, though it likewise lacks a certain precision and elegance of form, is an unquestionably brilliant and memorable story. What makes the difference? The answer is not difficult. The character of the father, another picture of the father of the author to be put beside Windy McPherson and Tom Appleton, is made to live through sheer force of literary creation. We can see him struggling to entertain his patrons, morbidly desirous of their attention and praise, a tragic spectacle of dismal and forlorn frustration. He is the simple-minded rustic impatient and maddened at the prospect of the endless ennui of continuous failure. The discrepancy between assets and aspirations, in his case, is the cause of a severe and eccentric reaction. The triumph of the egg is but the final touch to his tragedy. The closeness and intimacy of characterization, the extreme vividness of situation, provide us with a sense of reality, a duplication of the object

[93]

enhanced by the distillation of selection, that is the genuine source of esthetic appreciation. This is not so emphatically the case with *I Want to Know Why*. In the latter story, "the sense of reality," the concatenation and inevitability of action, are not so clear and cogent. A different, and more moving and subtle understanding of character is created by *The Triumph of the Egg*. Furthermore, the emotions awakened by the tortured pathology of the father, and his agonized endeavors at success and final admission of failure, are more varied and profound than those caused by the adventures of the mystified adolescent in *I Want to Know Why*. A reaction-barometer, the invention of the next generation, would prove this fact beyond question. *Out of Nowhere Into Nothing* is one of the best psychographic stories penned during this generation. Here the sex difficulties and afflictions of the stenographer, a Rosalind Westcott, and the flatly, boresomely married business man, a Walter Sayers, are subjected to a deep and piercing though somewhat mystical dissection. A clean and stimulating study in psychology, the story is none the less poetic. Here is a release, as we also found in *Winesburg, Ohio,* and for that matter can also find in *Jude the Obscure* and *The Portrait of the Artist as a Young Man,* from the bourgeois ethics of the Victorian era, which, despite the rise of the proletariat with its emphasis upon the very antithesis of this attitude, still hang on, with an oppressing and devastating ugliness, to our own esthetic culture. The realism is obtained not through coprolalic descriptions, appeals to trite and clammy sentimentalities, or wild orgiastic scenes of dubious reality, but through the calm, patient and lyrical method of emotional analysis, the sifting of varied nuances of feeling to their sexual origins, and the resolution of mental conflict into its component physical parts. The simple, almost universal struggle of this small-town girl is given just as serious study and consideration as the struggle of the ambitious Thane of Glamis. There is nothing patronizing, humanely condescending, in the author's approach to his subject, nothing but deep sympathy intensified by a yearning to pluck the problem from its roots and project it undistorted and naked before the mind's eye of the reader. We do not conclude from this that the story is perfect. It is not. More succinctness of narration would have heightened its esthetic value. Certain repetitions could have been avoided to good effect. A rearrangement of situation could easily have secured more successful dramatic effects, of mental as well as physical character, and given the story a finer and more abiding emotional appeal. But these deficiencies, necessary consequents of Anderson's unique habit of narration, are not sufficient to deprive the work of high literary value and significance.

Horses and Men, Anderson's latest volume of stories, contains one of the most odd collection of narratives that has appeared in America since Poe's *Tales of the Grotesque and Arabesque.* From the race-track *milieu* of *I'm a Fool* to the half-schizophrenic psychology of Edgar Wilson in *The Man's Story,* the best short story that Anderson thinks he has done, the collection breathes an air of strangeness and singularity. It is not the oddness of the grotesque that these stories embody, but an oddness of the real, a stressing of the unusual with only an occasional veering into the exaggerated and baroque. The characters, however, are never exquisite iridescent ghosts, as Van Wyck Brooks described the heroes of Poe and Hawthorne, but always living creatures, children of the soil, individuals whose beings beat with the passionate desires of life. *I'm a Fool,* a fresh attractive story, successful within its limits, captivates us by the subtlety of its climax. A trivial misstep, a thin breach of veracity, motivated by a temporary desire for self-apotheosis, is made the point of an exceptionally appealing, a deliciously flavored although not powerful story. It is the best "race-track" story Anderson has developed. Unfortunately, it does not have those qualities necessary to the evoking of a profound emotional reaction, the quality necessary to *power,* or the sublime, in a piece of art, and hence falls short of the vigor and beauty of such stories as

Ivan Ilyitch, The Black Monk, or *A Piece of String* —or even *Hands*. *Unused* comes closer to realizing that reaction, but its substance is so extended and diffuse, its divisions and multiplicity of situation so numerous, that the sense of unity, the refinement and crystallization of character, are rendered less effective than would have been the case had the same narrative been more evenly and compactly constructed. Its energy—and pulchritude—unluckily are potential rather than kinetic. *An Ohio Pagan,* a different type of story, does catch much of the moody mysticism of adolescence, the expectancy and strangeness of desire, the curious anticipation, peculiar to youth, of the unexplored. It is a striking, if not complete, picture. The sex-life of youth again is uncovered, and one is able to feel, through a delightful interweaving of symbolism with reality, something of the resurgent rush of adolescent emotion. There are few stories in our literature that have treated this theme with the same success. *The Man's Story* is a haunting study in schizophrenia. Despite an error in physiology which does not strengthen the realism and an excessive preoccupation with the weird and preternatural, the story has an enchanting sincerity and beauty. The phenomenal death of the woman should have been explained in a more satisfactory manner to sustain the realism.

"What the doctors said, who were put on the case afterwards, was that a cord or muscle, or something of the sort that controls the action of the heart, had been practically severed by the shot."

This is patently erroneous physiology. To one the least acquainted with the human body this is irritating and unconvincing. A cord or muscle of the heart could not have been severed since neither a cord nor muscle controls the heart; the heart is held in place by the great blood vessels, and its action is controlled by nerves, not by cords or muscle. Furthermore, an injury that would impair the nerve supply would tear the great blood vessels so that the person would bleed to death within a time much shorter than that lived by the woman after the shot. The story might have been explained, though perhaps not to our entire esthetic satisfaction, by stating that the bullet had injured one of the smaller blood vessels of the lung, but not of the heart. However, "the strange relationship of the two," the husband and wife, the queer abnormality of the former, his incommunicably vague and mystical verse, impregnated with an almost solipsistic pessimism, and his unnaturally callous attitude toward everything not intimate with his peculiar mental world, present sufficient material for an extraordinarily engaging and fascinating story. Here is a man trying to get closer to life, trying to understand its disillusionment and enigma, trying to know the strife and destiny of other souls besides his own, who nevertheless is everlastingly building himself inward instead of outward, and who is ever moving further and further away from all else save the inchoate fantasies of his mind. This, it seems, is the sorrowful and inevitable path of the mystic.

In a fragment of writing of Sherwood Anderson, taken from a letter to the author of this essay, we can discover an explanation of what may often have seemed, particularly in his novel *Many Marriages,* an afflicting inconsistency of attitude:

"What I have been striving for here is not a novel, in the ordinary sense in which that much abused word is used, but for a sort of fantasy. It is the same thing I was striving for in another work of mine, called *Many Marriages,* and that book caused confusion. Too many pornographic-minded people read it and I am afraid found in it a satisfaction I did not wish to give. . . . I am not trying to draw a picture of any actual life I have ever seen or have known anything about. It is all pure fantasy. If some of the settings are a bit realistic, do not let that confuse you. I have been caught in that confusion before. . . . Think of the figures as merely imagined people who, some months before I began writing of them, took up their residence in the house of my fancy. They lived there and certain things happened to them but these things did not happen in my life."

Many Marriages was condemned as fanciful and unreal. It certainly was—and is! According to Anderson's declaration it was meant to be nothing else. The violent strictures of most of the critics, therefore, were misguided heroics. The purpose of the book was misunderstood. The cause of this misapprehension, notwithstanding, is easily recognized, since all of Anderson's preceding efforts were adventures in realism. *Many Marriages* is a hazardous experiment. It is a cry of mystical protest. The clear social background of his earlier work is missing in this wild plunge into disembodied romanticism. The thin capriciousness of sex is woven into the strange grotesqueries of a dream. The story, however dazzling in substance, flutters high in mid-air, a radiant but unearthly phantom. The uncurved realities of human experience are transformed into the inextricable vagaries of a nightmare. The characters are of another world than that of reality, a world of monologic introspection, poetic rationalization, and dreamful theoretics. Judged as a piece of realism, then, the novel is a miserable fiasco. But, as we said, we must view it as a flare of fancy, a tribute to the fugitive emotions of the fanciful mind.

Many Marriages is saturated with sex-mysticism. It projects a feature of Anderson's own personality that is extremely fascinating and signal. There is a decisive difference, for example, between Thomas Hardy's approach to life and that of Sherwood Anderson. Hardy is content with intimate descriptions of emotion, the delineation of finely wrought tragedy based upon clear cause and effect sequence of action, while Anderson must probe deeper into the fluctuating shades of nervous response, and catch the little hints of soul-revelation that promise to lead to the very secret of individuality and human communication. This does not mean that Hardy and Anderson do not both view character with equal sympathy, understanding and not deprecating idiosyncrasy and perversity of action as we described earlier in this essay, but that their attitudes as to the finalism of character study are different in definiteness and motive. Hardy is the incorrigible pessimist, protesting at the puniness of life and its struggle, and yet cognizant of the futility of the protest. He is a fatalist, convinced of the inescapable tragedy of existence and impossibility of getting any closer to its mystery than the feeble sense of man will permit. Anderson is more of a romantic, despite the vivid realism of his earlier work, obsessed with the desire and hope of the mystic to get beyond the sensual knowledge of life into its very cause and essence.[20] Whether we seize upon Dionysius, the Areopagite, from whom western mysticism seems to have sprung, or Maurice Maeterlinck, the cynosure of

[20] *The Man in the Brown Coat* expresses this motive as clearly as *Many Marriages*.

the neo-mystics, the philosophic approach suffers little change of analysis or tactic. To the unmystical mind there are but two types of knowledge, knowledge of objects and knowledge of the relations between them, sensuous and intellectual knowledge. It is with such knowledge that the scientist contents himself, as also does an artist such as Thomas Hardy—or Giovanni Verga. The mystic, on the other hand, is discontent with this division. He does not deny the existence of perceptional and ideational knowledge, but maintains that the field of knowledge is not exhausted by this spurious dichotomy of its substance. There is for him —there must be to satisfy his passion for finality—a third kind of knowledge, an intuitional, spiritual knowledge that transcends the purely material forms. This third kind of knowledge, arising in the case of metaphysical mystics from the concepts of union, love, and ecstasy, can never be fully thought or expressed— hence its origin from the word *mio,* to keep your mouth closed—and yet mystics are forever trying to halo their experience in poetic raiment. This knowledge is the spiral gateway to the understanding of the very crux of life and the universe. Not all mystics are aware of the history or implications of their creed, nor do they concur in their personal sympathies and methods, yet in their dissatisfaction with the usual forms of knowledge, their disappointment with the descriptions and

final skepticism of science, their faith in a more intimate and illuminating kind of experience than the sensual and intellectual, they are undivided. Sherwood
Anderson, to return to our author, is no metaphysical
mystic, no mystic at all in what might be called the
common acceptance of the term. He does not dwell
upon the experience of union and ecstasy as did Words-
worth and Patmore, nor describe the beauty of a
seventh heaven as did Plotinus, nor even drift into descriptions of the Awakening of the Soul or the Invisible
Goodness as does Maeterlinck. Yet his attitude is often
profoundly mystical. He is not willing to accept descriptions of things, cold externalities, theories that
admit of no final solution, but must push deeper into
their very origin, caressing them, clothing them, making
them one with himself. In *Many Marriages,* for instance, he will not be a realist like Hardy, but must
erect a mental world of his own, where the fantastics of
a John Webster become natural and nature itself assumes a form incongruous with our experience. Realism, deriving its power from force of resemblance, cannot deal with "pure fantasy," with imagined individuals
detached from the salt of the soil; when it does it stultifies itself and ceases to be realism. The mystic, as we
said, sees in character a third kind of knowledge, a new
and more vivifying though scarcely describable substance, and when he lets his creations run the gamut of

his mind, they become more like spirits than men. The insufficiency of sense-contact, its meager revelations and tantalizing superficiality, drive the mystic to despair. He experiences a mad craving to know other souls than his own, know them in a more intimate way than the life of sense and intellect will allow. He is tortured by the prospect of solipsism. With Anderson, other people's souls become houses into which he must look and try to live; he must, as was the wish of Edgar Wilson, "cut and rip through all the ugly husks in which millions of lives are enclosed," . . . "take a row of houses standing on a street, tip them over, empty the people out of them, squeeze and compress all the people into one person and love that person." In *The Man in the Brown Coat* we find a queer contradiction:

"We keep a servant, but my wife often sweeps the floors, and she sometimes makes the bed in which we sleep together. We sit together in the evening, *but I do not know her*. I cannot shake myself out of myself. My wife is very gentle and she speaks softly, but she cannot come out of herself.

"My wife has gone out of the house. *She does not know that I know every little thought of her life*. I know what she thought when she was a child and walked in the streets of an Ohio town. *I have heard the voice of her mind*. I have heard the little voices. I heard the voice of fear crying when she was first

overtaken with passion and crawled into my arms."—
(Italics mine.)

In one place the man confesses he does not know his
wife, since he cannot get out of himself nor she out of
herself; but in the next paragraph he declares his
knowledge of every little thought of her life from the
time she was a child to the time of their love. This is
an intellectual inconsistency. It can only be explained
—and justified—by the mystic's retreat to a third kind
of knowledge that transcends "thought knowledge" as
air transcends the sea. Rich lyric prose gives *Many
Marriages,* to come back to this novel once again, a
strange, enamoring appeal. There is no fatal spell as
in *Pelleas and Melisande* to imprison the reader, no
green forest gloom to haunt and perturb him, no curious casketing of desire or exotic bedizening of figure.
A cool, lucid beauty characterizes many of the descriptions, and the whole book exudes a clean, naked odor
like that of flesh just emerging from the waters of a
rain-washed lake. The accusation of pornography is
despicably unjust. The symbolism of bodily contact
and infusion is done with a delicacy of diction quite
rare and discreet. John Webster's "rolling over the
floor at his daughter's feet and squirming about so that
he lay on his belly facing her," as ludicrously unreal

as his virgin altar and magic stone, is not without interest, though lacking in conviction.

It is when he gets away from reality, however, that Anderson becomes incoherent and mystifying, and fails to achieve the vividness and power of great art. In *Poor White* he came very close to writing the great American novel. Like his other extended efforts this book suffers from excessive lengthiness, and, in the last hundred pages, from a burdensome accumulation and repetition of detail. Had the last quarter of the novel been condensed, excepting the murder scene and the arrest of the paranoid harnessmaker, *Poor White* would stand out as the best realistic novel that America has produced. Like *Sister Carrie* it wabbles and staggers in the last lap, and finally accepts a regrettable but inevitable defeat. As it is, notwithstanding the dragging character of its closing chapters, it can easily be classified among the five best American novels. No American novel, not even the unmelodramatic parts of *The Octopus,* has caught the spirit of the changing west of the 70's, 80's, and early 90's, as has this work of Sherwood Anderson. The social environment from which Anderson himself has sprung is here portrayed with consummate skill and artistry. The evolution of an industrial age, the transformation of agricultural communities into manufacturing, the ideational changes wrought in the minds of the people seized thus between the fall of one and the rise of another civilization, are given an almost epical delineation. The birth of modern capitalism is seen in all of its early bloom and promise—and horrors.

"The crowds of people, who in the evenings walked out along Turner's Pike to look at the field with its long rows of sturdy young cabbages, moved restlessly about and talked of the new days. From the field they went along the railroad tracks to the site of the factory. The brick wall began to mount up into the sky. Machinery began to arrive and was housed under temporary sheds until the time when it could be installed. An advance horde of workmen came to town and new faces appeared on Main Street in the evening. The thing that was happening in Bidwell happened in towns all over the Middle West. Out through the coal and iron regions of Pennsylvania, into Ohio and Indiana, and on westward into the States bordering on the Mississippi River, industry crept. Gas and oil were discovered in Ohio and Indiana. Over night, towns grew into cities. A madness took hold of the minds of the people. Villages like Lima and Findlay, Ohio, and like Muncie and Anderson in Indiana, became small cities within a few weeks. To some of these places, so anxious were the people to get to them and to invest their money, excursion trains were run. Town lots that a few weeks before the discovery of oil or gas could have been bought for a few dollars sold for thousands. Wealth seemed to be spurting out of the very earth. On farms in Indiana and Ohio giant gas wells blew the drilling machinery out of the ground, and the fuel so essential to modern industrial development rushed into the open."

. . . "Farmers owning oil-producing land went to bed in the evening poor and owing money at the bank, and awoke in the morning rich. They moved into the towns and invested their money in the factories that sprang up everywhere. In one county in southern Michigan, over five hundred patents for woven wire farm fencing were taken out in one year, and almost every patent was a magnet about which a company for the manufacture of fence formed itself. A vast energy seemed to come out of the breast of the earth and infect the people. Thousands of the most energetic men of the Middle States were themselves out in forming companies, and when the companies failed, immediately formed others. In the fast-growing towns, men who were engaged in organizing companies representing a capital of millions lived in houses thrown hurriedly together by carpenters who, before the time of the great awakening, were engaged in building barns. It was a time of hideous architecture, a time when thought and learning paused. Without music, without poetry, without beauty in their lives or impulses, a whole people, full of the native energy and strength of lives lived in a new land, rushed pell-mell into a new age."

The hatred of the artisans for the incoming machinery is described with eloquent pathos. The tortured dreams of hundreds of tiny investors, men who had put their entire savings, no more than a few hundred dollars often, and yet all that they had, into the new projects, are pictured with a force no less moving and poignant. The instance of Joseph Wainsworth is extremely distinct and touching.

"The night had been dark and cloudy, but now the moon began to push its way through the clouds. Joe crawled over a pile of bricks and through a window into the building. He felt his way along the walls until he came to a mass of iron covered by a rubber blanket. He was sure it must be the lathe his money had bought, the machine that was to do the work of a hundred men and that was to make him comfortably rich in his old age. No one had spoken of any other machine having been brought in on the factory floor. Joe knelt on the floor and put his hands about the heavy iron legs of the machine. 'What a strong thing this is! It will not break easily,' he thought. *He had an impulse to do something he knew would be foolish, to kiss the iron legs of the machine or to say a prayer as he knelt before it.* Instead he got to his feet and, crawling out again through the window, went home. He felt renewed and full of new courage because of the experience of the night, but when he got to his own house and stood at the door outside, he heard his neighbor, David Chapman, a wheelwright who worked in Charlie Collins' wagon shop, praying in his bedroom before an open window. Joe listened for a moment, and, for some reason he couldn't understand, his new-found faith was destroyed by what he heard. David Chapman, a devout Methodist, was praying for Hugh McVey and for the success of his invention. Joe knew his neighbor had also invested his savings in the stock of the new company. He had thought that he alone was doubtful of success, but it was apparent that doubt had come also into the mind of the wheelwright. The pleading voice of the praying man, as it broke the stillness of the night, cut across and for the moment utterly destroyed his confidence. 'O God, help the man Hugh McVey to remove every obstacle that stands in his way,' David Chapman prayed. 'Make the plant-setting machine a success. Bring light into the dark places. O Lord, help Hugh McVey, *thy servant*, to build successfully the plant-setting machine.' "—(Italics mine.)

This, and other passages in *Poor White* are among the most beautiful things that Anderson has done. But he does not stop with a few patchy descriptions, a couple of paragraphs, interspersed to set off the narrative, as is the wont of the hasty and inferior novelist. He senses, and in the character of Judge Hanby indicates, the existence of class-struggle and predicts the future proletarian revolution.

" 'Well, there's going to be a new war here, he said. 'It won't be like the Civil War, just shooting off guns and killing people's bodies. At first it's going to be a war between individuals to see to what class a man must belong; then it is going to be a long silent war between classes, between those who have *and those who can't get*. It'll be the worst war of all.' "—(Italics mine.)

There is no romantic depiction here, no disturbing hero-worship, no vain soliloquizing and impossibilistic scheming as in *Marching Men*. The centralization of capital, with its necessary expulsion of the small enterprise, is keenly realized. And the attitude of the capitalist, the Steve Hunters, and Tom Butterworths, is not neglected. The division between the two classes is sketched clearly, without inaccuracy and sentimentality. The progress in socialist thought is noted well. It is the system and not the individual that is described as the cause of the diseased disparities of impulse and motive between the classes, and the source of the existing evils of society. Altogether the book presents a clear and effective picture of the social background of the Midwest during the last generation, from which arise and live its characters and situations, its atmosphere and movement.

The study of character also is more thorough and successful in *Poor White* than in any other of Anderson's novels; in fact it is surpassed only by the studies in *Winesburg, Ohio,* and a few in *The Triumph of the Egg* and *Horses and Men*. The life of Hugh McVey, "born in a little hole of a town stuck on a mudbank on the western shore of the Mississippi River," is traced with exquisite minuteness from his early association with his father and Sarah Shepard to his brilliant achievement as an inventor, and marriage with Clara Butterworth. It is after this point that the study begins to drag and lose much of its fascination. More discriminating selection of episode and greater brevity of description would have prevented this 'sharp diminution in interest and attractiveness. Clara Butterworth and her father, Steve Hunter, Kate Chancellor, Ed Hall, Rose McCoy, Judge Hanby, are all limned with careful distinction of individuality; suffering from neither exaggeration of impulse nor poverty of appeal they are unstilted, cogent creations. Next to Hugh McVey, the unprepossessingly modest, sex-puzzled inventor, however, the character of Joe Wainsworth, the harnessmaker, receives the finest treatment. In the development of this character is epitomized the embittered and futile struggle of the artisan with the invasion of the vast machinery of industrialism. The murder of Jim Gibson, a consequence of Wainsworth's inability to adjust himself to the new environment, is without question the best dramatic situation that Anderson has described. It is splendidly illuminating and effective. A kind of heavy monotony which had pervaded several of the chapters immediately preceding is relieved by the sharpness and vigor of this event. It is a radiant promise of what Sherwood Anderson will be able to do when his technique has become even more subtle and refined, and the element of the dramatic is introduced into his art with more frequency and elegance. In a final analysis, the emotional effect that a story aims at evoking is secured by its dramatic scenes, not its purely descriptive or expository. The appeal of the latter depends upon the strength and beauty of the former. Abstract the dramatic scenes from Sophocles, Shakespeare, Ibsen, Hardy, Dostoievsky—and what have you left? A colorless, immobile desiccated mass.

6

In an essay of Anderson's, which appeared some years ago, we can discover in a curious apology for crudity a singular reflection upon our uncorrelated American civilization. Our land is wide and loose and crude. Its surface and substance are shifting and chaotic. It is immature. Therefore the poetry and prose that we have must express this looseness and immaturity if they are to be an exact reflection of our nation. Sandburg and Carlos Williams accept and work upon this same theory. *Mid-American Chants,* for example, is an expression of this thesis, and it was upon this score particularly that Yvor Winters somewhat cleverly assailed it. The poems, adventures in *vers libre,* are neither remarkably good nor remarkably bad. They are pervaded with an unfleshy mysticism that unfortunately hovers too close to the ground to ever approach the aërial ecstasies of a Blake or a Shelley. There are poems like the *Song to the Lost Ones* that possess a kind of lyric beauty and also others that have a pregnant social meaning like *The Mid-American Prayer*:

> "You see, dear brothers of the world, I dream of new and more subtile loves for me and my men.
> My mind leaps forward and I think of the time when our hands, no longer fat, may touch even the lean dear hands of France, when we also have suffered and got back to prayer.
> . . . It is the time of the opening of doors.
> No talk now of what we can do for the old world.
> Talk and dream now of what the old world can bring to us—the true sense of real suffering out of which may come the sweeter brotherhood.
> God, lead us to the fields now. Suns for us and rains for us and a prayer for every growing thing.
> May our fields become our sacred places.
> May we have courage to choke with our man's hate him who would profit by the suffering of the world.
> May we strip ourself clean and go hungry that after this terrible story has passed our sacred fields may feed German, Jew, and Japanese.

> May the sound of enmity die in the groaning of
>   growing things in our fields.
> May we get to gods and the greater brotherhood
>   through growth springing out of the destruc-
>   tion of men.
> For all of Mid-America the greater prayer and
>   the birth of humbleness."

This does not have high poetic value, as one can
readily see, and yet we can perceive in it the sentiment
of our time, our grime-ridden, competition-strangling
America, and also the promise of our future song. We
must keep in mind Anderson's preface to the book:
"We do not sing but mutter in the darkness."

"In Middle-America men are awakening. Like awk-
ward and untrained boys we begin to turn towards
maturity and with our awakening we hunger for song.
But in our towns and fields there are few memory
haunted places. Here we stand in the roaring city
streets, on steaming coal heaps, in the shadow of factories from which come only the grinding roar of
machines. Our lips are cracked with dust and with
the heat of furnaces. We but mutter and feel our
way toward the promise of song.

"For this book of chants I ask that it be allowed
to stand stark against the background of my own place
and generation. Honest Americans will not demand
beauty that is not yet native to our cities and fields."

However crude and adolescent, these are songs of the

proletariat. They are devoted to no other class. No sickly bourgeois sentimentalism vitiates their content, no pandering to ancient muses, obsolete virtues, and dreary counsels halt their movement.

It should be noted at this point, as we approach the end of our analysis, that Anderson's preface, part of which is quoted in the preceding paragraph, takes a sharp stand on the side of realism. The chants are "to stand stark against the background of (his) own place and generation"; they are not to express the fanciful imagery and wind-wrought music of an eyrie-dwelling poet, but the rhythm of earthly reality and creation. The failure of many of the poems to achieve this end does not alter or mar the purpose. It is precisely this desire, this purpose, that is most fully and exquisitely achieved in *Winesburg, Ohio,* parts of *The Triumph of the Egg* and *Horses and Men,* and in *Poor White.* The pursuit of the mystical and the pursuit of the real are the dual elements to be discovered in the works of Sherwood Anderson. Of late they have come into active clash with each other. Both are interesting, both lyrical and striking, but the mystical is the less fundamental and enduring, the less universal, method of the two. *A Story Teller's Story* contains a mingling of the two elements, as would be necessary in the painting of a personality so introspectively mystical and yet so sensitively responsive to reality as that of Sherwood

Anderson. It is the clear clinging to reality, however, in the scenes given to description of his early western environment that enriches the first two books of the autobiography and endows it with an eloquence that almost equals the initial half of *Poor White*. Anderson's personality arises from this book clean and distinct, intensively glowing and active. With insurpassable naïveté he tells of his own craving for admiration, his childish mimickings of Bill Hart, his simple affection for beer—and dreams! Although the echoes of Anderson's *New Testament* have not ceased their reverberations in this volume, we still can note a growing clearness of vision and an increasing coherence of style through the book. We can see more clearly than ever how his work had to reflect the concept of the oppressed but rising proletariat, and could not have expressed any other class. We can realize how impossible it would have been for him to have written another tragedy like *Othello*, another novel like *Persuasion*, another story like *Mr. Whittaker's Retirement*. We can understand, then, why he wrote a *Poor White* and not *A House of Mirth; Hands*, and not *The King Is Dead, Long Live the King*. We can appreciate how a certain crudity of style can express the slowly refining but as yet unpolished character of the proletariat. And, finally, we can perceive in the work of this artist, who once was a house-painter, a workman in a factory, an advertising writer, and still is a painter of pictures, the spirit of the new generation beating racily and impatiently through every page that he pens. We can link him, in respect of concept if not of ultimate finish of form, with Thomas Hardy in England, Hauptmann and Ernest Toller in Germany, Verga in Italy, the Goncourts and Hamp in France, Hamsun in Norway, and Chekhov and Gorki in Russia.

THE IMPERMANENCY OF ESTHETIC VALUES

THERE is an esthetic theory, recently revived, which maintains that a work of art has a certain value, its genesis or environment notwithstanding. The advocates of this theory, in most part, are objectors to psychological and historical criticism. They wish to preserve the native purity of the esthetic experience. The scientific approach, they maintain, limits the capacity for appreciation. The scientific habit inhibits the artistic. In the work of Santayana, for instance, we discover a partial reflection of this tendency:

"It is evident that beauty is a species of value, and what we have said of value in general applies to this particular kind. A first approach to a definition of beauty has therefore been made by the exclusion of all intellectual judgments, all judgments of matter of fact or of relation. To substitute judgment of fact for judgment of value is a sign of pedantic and borrowed criticism. If we approach a work of art or nature scientifically, for the sake of its historical connection or proper classification, we do not approach it æsthetically. The discovery of its date, or of its author, may be otherwise interesting; it only remotely affects our esthetic appreciation by adding to the direct effect certain associations." [1]

A more extreme expression of this attitude can be found in some English estheticians of the nineties and in a number of contemporary critics engaged in discussion of this theme. A work of art, if it be great, has a value that neither weakens nor fluctuates, but is eternal. The vicissitudes of social evolution do not affect or ruffle its intrinsic excellence. The implication derived from this hypothesis, of course, is simple, and can be put in the form of the creed that art can rise above its environment—a contradiction and an absurdity.

In this brief analysis we shall show that a work of art does not possess a positive or absolute value; that its value is impermanent, depending upon the continuance of the environment that created it, and varies perceptibly with each change in social structure and imperceptibly with each change in immediate environment. In other words, the knowledge of the genesis of a piece of art is indispensable if we are to accurately determine its value at the time of consideration, and no criticism, therefore—and esthetics is but a particular form of criticism—can be satisfactorily complete if it is not at basis sociological.

Because misunderstandings can so easily and fre-

[1] *The Sense of Beauty,* George Santayana. Page 20.

quently intrude in such a discussion, we shall illustrate our position at considerable length. That esthetic conceptions change from age to age is a fact beyond dispute. What does this have to do with judgment and value? Does it necessitate sociological criticism? Obviously if esthetic concepts change, their change must be due to sociological processes; whether they be of idealistic or materialistic character does not alter their sociology. In this essay, rather than analyze and explain the causes for these changes, we shall devote our attention to the importance of the changes in the construction of any theory of the esthetic.

In the days of early civilizations there were books written, or at least composed verbally and tableted or penned later, that continue to have interest and value today. The Bible, the Homeric legends, the Egyptian *Book of the Dead*, the *Epic of Gilgamesh*—all of these can certainly be included in that group. For our purpose, however, it is better that we take only one of these books for our illustration. In this instance we shall employ the Bible. Now there is no question that on the whole this anthology of early Hebrew and Christian writings contains exalted sentiment, in many places fine description, poetry that often rises to the grandeur of an epic, shrewd psychology, even puns to inspirit the substance, and altogether furnishes an excellent picture of the dark and turbulent centuries in which it received its creation. And despite the immense intervals of years, rapturously exclaims the unscientific critic, beguiled by the idea of the absolute, the Bible remains the same glorious piece of literature that it was when originally written.

An important philosophic distinction is necessary at this point if we are not to be snared by the absolutist logic. The same object can have different effects at different times; a book, for example, entitled *Mr. M*, can have an effect B upon Miss Frana if read in a period of ecstasy, and the effect D if read in a period of discomfort and despondency, although the quality of the book has been a constant through both of the experiences. The same bullet going at the same velocity will have a different effect upon a stone wall than upon a sand-hill. These facts seem so clear and unmistakable that many may be irritated at their being presented in anything but a primer, and yet it is on refutation of just such logic that the utopian criticism is founded. Carrying our own logic to its inescapable conclusion, it means that an object may be significant at one period and insignificant at another, that it may have the value A at one time, the value F at another, and the value R at still another. A book which for us at twenty may have had the value A, at thirty deteriorates to the value E—the object in all of the cases having been a constant despite the fluctuation of judgment. With all of their simplicity the forcefulness of these facts can only be fully appreciated when the sociological or what are often called historical connections are comprehended. And from these very simple facts we derive the conclusion that the attribute of "great" or "value" is no more permanent than the rise and fall of social concepts. And further, that, since man's customs and ideas—which include his tastes and inclinations—vary with every change in his environment, there can be no judgment passed upon a work of art or science except in strict sociological terms.[2]   Esthetic criticism, then, must be sociological in fundament, or fail utterly of its purpose.

It is at this point that we can turn to our former illustration.   In consideration of what we said in the previous paragraph concerning the variations of esthetic judgment, and the impermanency of any im-

[2] For instance, the old illustration that $2+2$ equals 4, whether one be sick or well, should be finally exploded.   A number has more concreteness, because of the definite character of its associations, than a visual image or auditory sensation, but the process of perception is similar and the agreement or disagreement as to the nature of the impression is dependent equally upon the state of the body and mind at the time of perception.   To a man suffering with paresis, 2 and 2 may make eleven or seven or five, just as to a man afflicted with toothache a fascinating novel of genuine quality may be dull and of little value.   The matter of numbers, therefore, is conditioned just as distinctly by the state of the perceiving organism as the matter of dramatic criticism, except that numbers, which are more definite coördinates and are without the intertwining connotations of dramatic impressions, have acquired an acceptability, or objectivity, that no coördinates in the judgment of the drama as yet have been able to secure.

mediate criticism, can we say that the Bible to its
readers is the same "glorious piece of literature" that
it was to its readers in the centuries of its composition
or the religious centuries that followed the Christian
era?   To say that it is would be to say that man's
customs and ideas do not change with alterations in
environment, which, of course, is an extremity into the
ridiculous.   Men living today under the scientific and
industrial conditions of the twentieth century or the
latter part of the nineteenth, have different conceptions
than men of the early centuries preceding and following
the advent of the Christian creed, and their respective
attitudes toward things religious afford no greater contrast than their attitudes towards things ethical and
scientific.   The men who read the Bible in 500 A. D.
were very different from the men who read the Bible
in 1925; the frame of mind in which the men of the
former age approached the same book was very different from the frame of mind in which the men of the
latter age make their approach.   It is impossible that
the same book, although a constant in itself, could re-
ceive the same evaluation in both periods, since it was
affecting organisms that had experienced change in
their very faculties for evaluation, and whose very
coördinates from which their evaluations were made,
had veered.   Put in other terms—merely for conven-
ience we may make them mathematical—the Bible to

the man of the Middle Ages, when the human mind was steeped in superstition and magic and retreated in awe before the slightest physical anomaly, may have had a value of 98, using one hundred as the basis, while to men of today, when the human mind is accustomed to scientific thinking and is less moved by legerdemain and superstition, it may have a value of but 74. These figures are only used to denote change in evaluations due to change in the environment of the evaluator.

The Greek tragedies, an advance in technical construction over the literature of the Hebrews and Christians, do not supply any contradiction to this issue. We can still vividly appreciate the poetic descriptions of the sacrifice of Polyxena and the anguish of Antigone, and yet not derive great fascination from the chorus or other devices the Greeks used to introduce wit and satire, or be deeply affected by the tribulations of the gods, or moved by situations that too often lack the inevitability which modern art must possess in order to be excellent. In comparison with the art of other periods we may even give these tragedies an evaluation that is higher than those which was accorded them during the period in which they were staged, although the judgment is made from different coördinates than the ones used in the instance of the original judgment, and in no way disturb the validity of our thesis. The plain fact is that we appreciate the tragedies in an historical sense, just as we approach them in an historical manner. To one acquainted with the brilliance and profundity of Hellenic culture these tragedies have a meaning that is almost entirely ▐▐ to the contemporary layman. It should be clear ▐▐ this alone, if no other evidence were offered, that appreciation or criticism of Greek tragedy or Roman tragedy, or any ancient or non-contemporary piece of art, cannot be legitimate if it disregard the significance of the sociological element. A denizen of the twentieth century whose body and mind have been formed by the environment of an industrial age cannot approach the literature of an agricultural period so undeveloped and remote as that of ancient Greece, and expect to secure the same understanding and enjoyment from it as did the early Greeks themselves unless his attitude be profoundly historical and sociological. And however historical be his attitude, it can never approximate in even the crudest fashion that of the real contemporaries any more than the inhabitants of Mars, were they to land upon this earth and acquire all the historical data necessary to an understanding of our past and present, would be able to appreciate, in the way that we do, the esthetics of our planet.

Another illustration will advance our point further and reinforce its cogency. This time we shall take as an example a classic of the fifteenth century, the age when feudalism, with its trappings of chivalry and medieval magic, was at its zenith. Malory's *Morte d'Arthur*, a legendary epic of Arthur and his Round Table, is said to have first come out in the year 1485, just at the end of the War of the Roses. At the time that it appeared it certainly was valued differently by its readers, comparatively few though they were, than it is valued today. Until the disappearance of feudalism it retained a value that was quite constant, and had the system of feudalism been permanent its value would never have fluctuated except as minor changes in the system determined. Its value during the period of feudalism, to continue our simple scheme of evaluation, we may set at 90; this value, of course, changed as soon as feudalism began to alter and decline and new ideas and types of art [3] began to spring up, and with the introduction of industry and the development of capitalism the change became more pronounced and abrupt. It is safe to say at the present time that if *Morte d'Arthur* had a value of 90 during the fifteenth century its value now is about 60. In noting this reduction we do not mean to conclude that this epic is not of historical importance—assuredly it is—but that its value to the present age, with new organization, ideas and conceptions, and new system of coördinates, is not and could not be the same as the value it had for

[3] See the article, *Sociological Criticism of Literature.*

[127]

the fifteenth century. Different systems of social structure produce different reactions in men, change the demands of the mind in every field in which it is occupied, political, economic, ethical, and esthetic, and that which expressed and satisfied one age does not and cannot in the same precise and complete sense satisfy another.

That Malory's *Morte d'Arthur* does not have the same value for us today that it had five centuries ago is a statement that no scientific critic would contest, which of course is proof of the variation of values according to the change of social systems from which they arise, and of the necessity of the sociological approach in criticism of art. The stupidity of the statement, then, that "if we approach a work of art or nature scientifically, for the sake of its historical connections or proper classification we do not approach it esthetically" is as painfully apparent as the stupidity of the idea that a work of art has a certain steady value regardless of its genesis or environment. And continuing further, any position in esthetics that maintains that "whatever course history may take, the question of what is desirable is not affected," [4] which is but a ramification of the same theory, is but a shadowy evasion of the very basis of any philosophy of the esthetic.

[4] George Santayana—*The Sense of Beauty.* Pages 26, 27.

If we advance later in the period of feudalism and seize upon one of the Elizabethan dramas as an illustration we are certain to invite sharp and scorching attack. We shall tread cautiously at first, however, in order not to offend too abruptly the boxed-in sensibilities of the fossilized professorial critic and the reckless temperament of the impressionist.

Suppose we take Cyril Tourneur's *The Revenger's Tragedy* for an initial example. Here we have a tragedy that certainly is typically Elizabethan with its characteristic villain, one feature which fortunately Shakespeare in large part avoided, its lurid category of crimes, with murders, deaths, and suicides interspersed like so many scarlet suns, its appeal to guise and unconvincing duplicity, and all phrased in blank verse which Swinburne said for "commanding power and purity, in positive instinct of expression and direct eloquence of inspiration stands alone in the next rank to Shakespeare." This play unquestionably retains an historical interest that is quite striking and unique, and reading it in the twentieth century, cognizant of the new criteria of art composition, is neither a tiresome nor an unstimulating task. Yet the drama has a different value to us today than it had in 1607 when it was first printed. The feudal equipment is no longer to our taste and arouses in us question rather than satisfaction with the essence of the theme. The vengeful villain no longer awakens serious terror and pathos. The underlying motive of the plot, with all of its curious and often irritating involutions, convincing to the Elizabethan audiences, fails to impress us as realism of sound and genuine character. The heroic gestures of the protagonist are almost as laughable as they are exaggerated. The delineation of character is poor and ineffectual. Dramatic intensity is secured by scenes that flow with no inevitability from those that precede, and that are no more convincing in substance than those of the ordinary melodrama of the twentieth century. Then what remains? Poetry! Exquisite, rare, and soaring blank verse; magnificent imagery, sharply turned phrases that delight and please the ear, that distinguish the speaker and at moments almost endow unreality of action with the masque of reality. A drama that at one time, structurally considered—and structure is one of the basic coördinates of esthetics— had a value of, let us say, 88, in the twentieth century, with the decease of feudalism and the rise of a scientific, industrial society, built upon the supremacy of the bourgeois, has but a value of 75, and that value is retained primarily because of the exceptional elegance of phrase and rhythm.

Is Shakespeare immune from such criticism? Not in the least! In his plays we find the same feudal accoutrements, the same heroic gestures, in many instances the same weakness of plot, redeemed, however, by finer depiction of character and in frequent cases thoroughly convincing scenes of "dramatic intensity." To maintain that Shakespeare's plays when enacted today have the same capacity to convince that they possessed in the sixteenth, seventeenth, and eighteenth centuries, would be a veritable *reductio ad absurdum*. We are certainly still close enough to the period of feudalism to be able to appreciate something of the tribulations of a king and the ambitions of a lord, the struggle for thrones and empires, although our interest and sympathy with the heavenly powers, cherubim and seraphim live but in a twilight state of recollection. At one time, not many centuries ago, we could have been and were stimulated and attracted by the war of the heavenly host, a theme that today not only rests purely in recollection but is quite void of appeal. *The time will come likewise, with successive changes in society, when the struggle of emperors and lords, the consequences of the strifes and aspirations of royalty, will be as remote and unfascinating as the conflicts of the angelic hierarchy,* and with the coming of this period the value of Shakespeare's dramas, like all others expressing the attitude of feudalism, will suffer distinct diminution in value. Bernard Shaw understood the issue when he said, in way of serious and solemn stricture, that Shakespeare contributed

not a single idea that was in advance of his generation. One cannot hold accountable an artist for such
inadequacy for the simple reason that an author can
but express those ideas that come to him from his
environment, and since Shakespeare was enmeshed in
feudal politics, ethics, and metaphysics, he surely could
not but express the ideas of feudalism. The bourgeois
class did not acquire marked strength in England until
the seventeenth century, and the proletariat remained
entirely uncrystallized until the nineteenth. It is foolish, therefore, to attack Shakespeare for his numerous
disparagements of both bourgeois and proletarian, his
contempt for the "hempen-homespuns," the "mechanic
slaves with greasy aprons" and his disdain for that
desired by the "general will." In plain words it is
futile to try to excuse Shakespeare's attitude toward
the working man; the attitude is clear and cannot be
obscured by sophistical reasoning or pleas of poetic
license. The aristocratic conception of tragedy was a
feudal conception and Shakespeare not only observed
its regulations but believed as firmly in its accuracy
as we in the twentieth century believe in its inaccuracy.
Changes in social conditions, due to the introduction
of machinery, have changed the conceptions with the
necessary result that today Shakespeare's attitude
toward the working man, and his depiction of his characteristics, has far less value than it had in the fifteenth

[132]

and sixteenth centuries. This means, of course, that his dramas as a whole, and no critic can judge a drama aside from the social forces that created it, have a different value today than they had during the whole period of feudalism. This fact is so clear that we need not make any numerical evaluations, as we did in our previous instances, in order to emphasize the difference.

The history of the *tragedie bourgeoise* furnishes an even more singular instance of such variations of value. We could take Lillo's *The London Merchant,* Lessing's *Sarah Simpson,* or the dramas of Diderot or Nivelle de la Chaussee, in proof of our point in this reference. We shall take *The London Merchant* this time. Although *The Orphan* and *The Fatal Marriage* had preceded it, this play of Lillo's marked a revolution in English theatrics. It signified the real beginning of the *tragedie bourgeoise* in England. The play was enthusiastically praised by Pope, Rousseau, Marmontel, Lessing, Goethe, Schiller, and Diderot who ranked it beside the tragedies of Sophocles and Euripides, and was acted by famous actors and actresses, including Mrs. Siddons, Charles Kemble and Sir Henry Irving, for many generations. At the time when *The London Merchant* appeared, then, and during the year when bourgeois supremacy was undisturbed by the rise of the proletariat, and the science of esthetics had not made the advances that characterized its existence in the nineteenth and twentieth centuries, this play had a value we may say of 90; today or in the last three-quarters of the century previous, with the changes in society that have followed the strengthening and organization of the proletariat, and the necessary esthetic changes flowing from this social change, the play has a value of only, say, 60. The situations in *The London Merchant* are as grotesquely unconvincing as many of those in *The Revenger's Tragedy,* and the characterization is neither so fine nor subtle. Yet at the time the play was staged, the attitude of critics, formed by the early rise of the bourgeois and the social forces concomitant with this, was of such a character as to rate it far higher than the attitude of later critics, formed by a new change in social conditions, would permit. This change, nevertheless, as we have seen, is but in consonance with the entire history of esthetic theory and practice.

Contemporary esthetics, however, provide us with a still more complete and interesting example of the fluctuation of esthetic values according to change of social environment. In 1917 a revolution occurred in Russia which has disturbed the equanimity of the world. For over seven years, against obstacles seemingly insuperable, the Bolsheviki have ruled Russia and labored toward the institution of proletarian culture. The significance of the phrase "proletarian culture" is realized by but few critics. For the purpose of this essay it is not necessary to discuss the basis and theories of proletarian art, save to say that it means the ascendancy of the proletarian as the subject for esthetic treatment, the decline of the bourgeois conception and the final burial of the feudal or aristocratic. The Bolsheviki have taken a quite severe stand toward bourgeois esthetics. Not over ten months ago we learned that the books of Tolstoi, Turgenev, and others have been banned from the libraries and forbidden to the populace; [5] the reason offered in explanation of the act was that the works of these authors represent bourgeois, not proletarian, culture. The action, we may declare, was harsh and reckless, but it is of unique, indeed incalculable, significance. It means that with the advent of proletarian governments—and the advance of proletarian parties in England, France, Norway, and Germany is sufficient portent of what is to come—esthetic concepts will again change, and what yesterday was the pride of a literary civilization, tomorrow will become a curious but

[5] This statement was for a time denied by the communist press, but just recently has been affirmed by Madame Lenin in the April 9th issue of the *Pravda*. In the list of proscribed volumes were such books as *Anna Karenina, War and Peace,* and *Resurrection* of Tolstoi, *Oblomov* by Goncharov, *Fathers and Children,* and *Rudin* by Turgenev, *The Idiot* and *The Possessed* by Dostoievski, and in addition to these, many of Gregorovitch's works were condemned, and in the same category went a host of the productions of Andreyev and Gussiev-Orenburgsky.

fragile and withering vestige. This seems so ridiculous and impossible to us now, but so did the concept of democracy seem to the aristocracy of feudalism. Russia today is a living example of what may occur to esthetic standards within a few generations. It is not a matter of dislike or preference but of eventuality; we may dislike intensely what has occurred and condemn the Bolsheviki as "parvenu estheticians," as some have done, but the strength of the example and the trend of society are there just as inevitably. Under a proletarian culture, for instance, Tolstoi's works, which, under the feudal regime of Russia and to the bourgeois societies of the farther Occident possessed a rating of, let us say, 90, would be reduced perhaps to a value of less than 60. The Victorian novels devoted to the promotion and praise of bourgeois virtues, so inestimably significant to the bourgeois society of which they were an inseparable part, will be viewed as the productions of an age from which man has fortunately emerged, and their rating will be decisively different from that which they originally had, or at the present time possess. No matter how gradual this process its importance cannot be dismissed with a gesture. To see *David Copperfield*, which today we may give a value of 85, classified as bourgeois and forced to a position of 45, is an event that will cause fear and alarm to more than one of our tender-minded intellectual folk. Of course it is impossible to say exactly what change in evaluations will take place, but the nature of their change to any sociologist, or scientific critic, is not difficult to foresee.

Our conclusions, therefore, are clear and inescapable. There is nothing of the absolute in esthetic judgments, nothing that is not subject to the vicissitudes of social environment. A critical judgment could only be ultimately permanent, considered in historical perspective, if the ideas and customs of man, the concepts by which he reasons, the social organization from which these ideas, customs, and concepts arise, were static, and not in the state of flux that Heraclitus so long ago perceived, that the Hindus rapturously worship, and that Hegel, Buckle, Marx, and Darwin so eloquently proved. Every change in environment, be it the result of invention or discovery, or of a carefully or recklessly planned method of reconstruction, must inevitably alter the nature and value of the judgments which were made previously under another environment. In other words men are not the same in all ages; they differ widely and significantly. The whole theory of evolution attests to this fact. No esthetic object, or any other object therefore, can be satisfactorily approached and understood, and this includes the element of esthetic appreciation, except through the scientific, sociological method. The genesis or environment of a piece of art is indispensable to an understanding of its effect upon its observers. Knowledge of origins affects immediately, not remotely, our esthetic experience. And finally the entire problem of values is so knit into the texture of society that no judgment of an art-object can be made except in terms of the social-structure, and the permanency of that judgment is dependent upon the permanency of the social structure from which the judgment arose. In no other way can the oscillation and relativity of esthetic values be explained.

PROLETARIAN ART

THE proletarian motif has introduced a new psychological element into art. Artistic substance becomes imbued with a freshness and a universality that classical art could never attain. The interwoven dependence of one form of life upon another, the collective unity of the human race, become realities pregnant with esthetic as well as social significance. The distinction of caste, a vestigial characteristic of contemporary civilization, is already fading with the progress of the proletarian concept. In clear and definite contrast, bourgeois concepts are starting to shake and totter as the civilization which created them is gradually approaching its destruction. The uncertainties and irrational strangeness of modern art, the wild, frenetic and unrhythmical flow of line, color, and verse, the distortionate visions of the modern mystic, are all unequivocal manifestations of the moribund state of the prevailing bourgeois society and culture. The febrile revolt against the slavishly acquisitive economics of the bourgeois system, its hypocrisies of political principle, its stultifying puritanic ethics, headed by a wing of the bourgeois itself, as well as by the fuglemen of the proletariat, are further illustrations of just how this trend is shaping itself in literature and philosophy. The superficiality of this anti-bourgeois criticism, fostered in America by men like Mencken and Babbitt, does not obscure its importance as an index to our social disintegration. It is no less signal than the cry of the small bourgeois, caught in the vice of a rapidly centralizing society, against the oppression of their rights and the usurpation of their enterprise by the higher strata of their own class. All point inevitably in the same direction.

"Hatred of the bourgeoisie is the beginning of virtue," the Flaubertian proclamation of the nineteenth century, vigorously expresses the rebellious attitude of at least two generations. With the present generation the meaning of the proclamation has become more clarified; social concentration has given it a more crystallized form, a sharp, forceful definiteness, and an expression clearer if not more refined, subtler if not more powerful. Professor Sherman, the W. D. Howells of our generation, in his essay "The National Genius," has contended that contemporary divergences from the bourgeois conceptions are but the manifestations of a recalcitrant youth—futile "bucking of the national genius." This is a blind and shallow evasion. The violent anti-bourgeois attack of men like Dreiser and Anderson in America, Joyce in Ireland, Verhaeren in Belgium, Toller in Germany, not to mention a host of

[140]

others, does not express the vaporous eccentricity of
the immature or the undefined aspirations of the
utopian. There is a social-consciousness, imperceptible
perhaps to the artists themselves, present in the works
of these men that is more moving than the anemic art
of the fading bourgeois. The soft, purring music
of an Emily Dickinson could no more express the spirit
of our age than the staccato rhythms, the vivid literali-
ties, the rhymeless clamorings of a Sandburg could have
expressed the attitude of hers. The Lizette Reeses,
gentle, one-stringed artists of an evanescing *genre,* are
retreating before the rushing cadences of a changing
civilization.

It is not the function of a critic to declare the poetry
of a Lizette Reese infinitesmal in value because it is
unsucculent of the spirit of the rising generation, but
to point out that it should be studied in relation to its
own class, of which it is a part, and evaluated in accordance with the type of art it represents. But it is
as risibly fallacious of the Shermans to maintain that
we must cling to this type of lyricism, this moody se-
questration of impulse and vain shadowing of reality,
as it was of Rousseau to argue that salvation was to be
secured only by a return to the primeval. However,
it is true that every state of society must have its conservative, "reminiscent" element, devoted to a perpetuation of the *status quo,* with an additional craving for

the "finer" gold of yesterday, and Professor Sherman, with his compeers, Professors Moore and Babbitt, are but a vital exemplification of this attitude. No matter how inevitable, this approach is a viciously undermining influence. It is far more to be deplored than the sciolistic strictures of a Henry Mencken or the vorticistic ejaculations of an Ezra Pound. Yet it is this polluted type of criticism that is propagated by our educators throughout the country, in the institutions of California, the Mid-West, and the fringe of the Atlantic. In fact, it is devastatingly unubiquitous.

It is only the birth of a literature which represents the proletarian concept that gives promise of an enduring opposition. The poetry of Sandburg and Masters, the dramas of Eugene O'Neill, the fiction of Anderson, Dreiser, and, to an extent, that of Willa Cather and Sinclair Lewis, are evidences of this new trend. Whitman was perhaps the first to voice it in America, and Frank Norris, Stephen Crane, and, to a lesser degree, Graham Phillips were its continuators. Since the war it has had a rapid, intensively poignant growth.

It is at this point that we must indicate more exactly the features of the proletarian concept as distinct from the bourgeois and aristocratic. We discover with proletarian art the growth of a new esthetic. The clash of class-psychologies has precipitated a revolution in art values and criteria. In literature, for instance, the working man, as distinguished from the noble, the merchant and the *magister,* becomes a figure essential to its evolution; tragedies formerly spun about the episodic futilities of royalty, the failures of gamesters and business men, now include the disasters of the proletariat. The proletarian is visualized as no less a hero than the knight or financier. The ethics of the bourgeois, by the very process of social antithesis, so adequately illustrated by Hegel and Plechanoff, are repudiated by the evolving proletariat. *Virtues like honesty and chastity, denuded of their verbal veneer and deceptive duality of application, no longer become the embodiment of greatness in character and the source of profound emotional appeal.* The novels of Flaubert, Zola, Hamsun, Anderson, Dreiser, Willa Cather, all have successfully abandoned such *motifs.* The esthetic apotheosis of such virtues belonged to the day of the bourgeois novel, the day of *The Scarlet Letter* and *Adam Blair.* The attitude toward the whole problem of sex, in line with the same trend of social antithesis, has become unfettered of bourgeois prejudice and is seeking out toward a more living and comprehensive expression. The sermonical novel, so dominant and widely in vogue during the heyday of the Victorians, with the rise of the proletariat has become

obsolescent. The bourgeois attitude toward the obli-
quities and perversities of human action, the reverse
of intelligent and generous, becomes understandable
and magnanimous when transformed into the proletarian.[1] Crime is conceived as a product of conditions
and not of the innate wickedness of human nature.
Condemnation is turned into pity, and punishment into
treatment.[2] A Draco becomes a Ferri, and a judge
becomes a physician. Evil in characters is pictured
without the attempt to make them hideous, but to reveal the injustice of a social system or the iniquity of
circumstance. The Heeps, Murdstones, Draculas,
Dunsey Casses, Judases, and their antitheses the Evan-
gelines, Agneses, Pauls, and Virginias, are transmogri-
fied into creations that are less despicable or less perfect
but more convincing and real. The whole proletarian
trend is toward a deeper realism, pruned of ornamental
trappings, rugged almost with its undecorated exterior
and uncurved sharpness of delineation, and fully cognizant of the social origin and meaning of action.

[1] This does not mean that certain exigencies do not demand rigid,
often brutal, tactics of an uncrystallized proletariat, but that the
understanding and magnanimity noted are the necessary social consequents of the approaching change in our economic structure. The
temporary defection from such an attitude, occasioned by a political
revolution or economic emergency, in this stage of social evolution,
is no argument against the reality of the trend and the unmistakable
nature of its final direction.

[2] See Ferri's *Criminal Sociology*, and Blatchford's *Not Guilty*.

This realism toward which proletarian art is driving in its annihilation of class-distinctions possesses a comprehensiveness of content, singularly communistic in its development. Contrary to the usual belief there is no unilaterality in the attitude, considered in its fullness, no puffery of a single group at the expense of others except as an immediate situation in society might necessitate—as at the present time—but the promise of a complete synthesis of them all. Its philosophy aims toward a universality, but not uniformity, of substance. Its appeal is exclusive of no nation, no race, no class. Whitman expressed this sentiment eloquently:

"Literature is big only in one way—when used as an aid in the growth of the humanities—a furthering of the cause of the masses—a means whereby men may be revealed to each other as brothers."

His poems are mellifluous with the same strain:

"One's Self I sing—a simple, separate Person;
    Yet utter the word Democratic, the word En
    Masse."

Of the greatness of the destiny of the mass he sings, incessantly, audaciously. Their sufferings become part of his own, their protest is his protest; their failures his failures—he is "the hounded slave that flags in the race, leans by the fence, blowing, covered with sweat," he the "mashed fireman with breast-bone broken," "the

[145]

youngster taken for larceny," "the common prostitute."
There is a kind of mystical mergence of impulse in
these verses, a romantic projection of self, that is a
vivid reflection of the creeping spirit of the proletariat
during the latter half of the nineteenth century. Of
the coming of equality, the unconscious aim of the approaching upheaval of classes, he writes with courageous enthusiasm:

> "In all people I see myself—none more, and not
> a barleycorn less,
> And the good or bad I say of myself I say of
> them.
> Oh, strongly reflect all except Democracy! . . .
> Oh, to build for that which builds for man-
> kind. . . .
> Oh, workmen and workwomen forever for me!
> Oh, farmers and sailors! Oh, drivers of horses
> forever for me!
> Oh, equality! Oh, organic compacts! I am
> come to be your born poet."

Were we to become in our sociology as idealistic as
Tugan-Baranovsky we might say that this poetry of
Whitman's is a "spiritual" building upon the economic
structure, but it is far more accurate though prosaic
to use the words of Plechanoff and to state that it is
simply the expression of a mind that grasped, through

[146]

a favorable collocation of stimuli, "the meaning of the new generating social relations."

If for a moment we turn to the works of Emerson, the American apostle of the 1830's, 40's, and 50's, we shall discover an illuminating contrast.[3] Emerson wrote when capitalism was just beginning to stretch its vast tentacles across the country; the railroads were undeveloped, communication was slight, the West was still uninvaded by the countless hordes that swept across its heart following the gold rush of '49, and the promise of Eldorados continued to gleam like beguiling will-o'-the-wisps. Industry had scarcely begun to centralize, cities had yet to thicken and reek with the dun smoke of multiplying factories, and individual enterprise had still the chance of temporary survival and success. The individual, therefore, had greater opportunity, greater freedom. The limitation and oppression of an interwoven industrial system had yet to encompass him. The necessary interdependence of individuals had yet to be emphasized. Hegiras like that of Thoreau did not seem egregious anomalies. The philosophic attitude, as a consequence, was logically individualistic. Emerson's works are a reflection of this early, almost golden, age of capitalism—capitalism

[3] Although Emerson lived until 1882, the 30's, 40's, and 50's were the formative years of his life, the years that determined the nature of his philosophy.

[147]

fresh with the hope of an unending spring. His preachings of "self-reliance," the virtue of isolation, the strength of individual principle, all infused with a transcendental essence, are the accurate manifestations of the sociology of this period. The "Trust thyself" motto, the sesame of the Emersonian metaphysic, is but the same idea differently phrased.

"It is only as a man puts off all foreign support and stands alone that I see him to be strong and to prevail. He is weaker by every recruit to his banner. Is not a man better than a town? Ask nothing of men, and, in the endless mutation, thou only firm column must presently appear the upholder of all that surrounds thee." [4]

There is not the kind of democracy in Emerson that there is in Whitman. They represent different generations, different economic and social epochs, different phases of class evolution. Emerson is the idolater of great men, not the genuine lover of the "prostitute" and "carpenter." He is the herald of individual not social development. The importance of the socialization of labor, the *sine qua non* of the later stages of capitalism, he did not see and hence could not appreciate. During the period of his apogee the proletariat

[4] Essay on Self-Reliance.

was undefined, a groping, unsettled group. White slavery had just disappeared in 1831.

"The poor and low find some amends to their immense moral capacity, for their acquiescence in a political and social inferiority. They are content to be brushed like flies from the path of a great person, so that justice shall be done by him to that common nature which it is the dearest desire of all to see enlarged and glorified. They sun themselves in the great man's light, and feel it to be their own element."

This, the song of the bourgeois, was unchallenged until the few feverish years preceding the Civil War. It was Whitman whose rhythms rose in protest. It was Whitman, but fifteen years younger than Emerson, who put the muffled music of the swelling proletariat into poetry. He was expressing another phase of capitalism, another generation, *another class*. His poetry marked the rise of our proletariat, the first coming of our proletarian art. Its divergence from the bourgeois trend is apparent without further description. It is the dividing line of a literary epoch.

In Whitman there remained but few of the vestiges of the earlier concept, and these too are passing with the intensification of the proletariat and the gradual refinement of proletarian art. In Germany and Russia the plunge into the new art has been preternaturally violent and rapid. At times this art has possessed a ferocity verging on madness. Toller, Hasenclever, Libedinsky—these are its stars. But they are its promise, not its fulfillment.

FRAGMENTS FROM A CRITIQUE OF
AMERICAN CRITICISM

THE WISDOM OF THREE CRITICS
WOODBERRY, SPINGARN, SHERMAN

THE tradition of American criticism is quixotically incongruous. From the critical excursions on clothes and religion of Nathaniel Ward, the urbane superficialities of Lowell, the apologetic dissensions of Howells to the pseudo-clarifying analyses of Spingarn, Brownell, and Sherman, criticism in America has been notably vague, uncorrelated, and ineffectual. Poe is the only exception that can be cited. And even here, with the material of Poe, we meet with troubled eccentricity, brash denigrations and capricious enthusiasms often repented in moments of cooler contemplation. Poe's method of dissection not unrarely was mathematically accurate, and was executed with unexcelled artistry and logical brilliance. More often, however, particularly when his criticism was removed from the matter of abstract principle and ratiocination, he was concerned, as Hennequin has shown, with pettinesses, dealing with the infinitesimal and ephemeral, that befit a reviewer rather than a critic. It is certain also that his critical theory, except in the analysis of poetry, never rose beyond the immediate and never included aught of the interaction of social forces that go to make the concepts and trend of a literature. However acute, and its acuteness was unfortunately limited to a narrow area, Poe's criticism was not comprehensive. No spirit of coördination permeated and beautified its substance. In fact America has had no "coördinating mind" in the field of literary criticism. No Plechanoff, Taine, or Brunetière has sprung from our soil; not even a penetrating and wide-sympathied intellect such as that of Georg Brandes, or of Anatole France, or even of that of Remy de Gourmont or J. M. Robertson has punctuated our horizon.

If we seize upon American criticism of today we shall perceive, in large part, a series of shallow rationalizations, a puffery of the inessential, a confused scribbling about morality, a blathery defense of slapstick emotionalism, a projection of a *new* approach that antedates Goethe, onslaughts on the business man's psychology, sedate apologies for traditions, archæological remnants of deceased social epochs, denunciations of psychological and historical esthetics, vain retreats to Horace and Aristotle, all subsidized by a wealth of allusion and imagery but a paucity of insight and analysis. This critical myopia is not confined to any one group, moral or amoral, professorial or pseudo-esthetic. If, for a moment, we take the work of Professor Woodberry we shall see with more clarity precisely what is meant. In his essay *Two Phases of Criticism, Historical and Esthetic,* he defends the historical method for sixteen pages—where but in the American Critical Debate would such a defense be other than trivial?—proudly proclaiming that we cannot understand the art of the past without historical knowledge and discrimination, that historical criticism is the source by which the object is made clearer and more meaningful. Then, in the latter part of the essay, which is devoted to esthetic criticism, he wanders into nebulous discussions of universals, the faculties of the soul, and the "communion of saints," and concludes in a mist of confusion characteristic of a religious sermon:

"The artistic life (is one) that one shares in the soul universal, the common soul of mankind which yet is manifest only in individuals and their concrete works. Art, like life, has its own material being in the concrete, but the spiritual being of both is in the universal."[1]

The preceding quotation in illustration of the esthetic approach to life and the material of art is surpassed only by the unconscious cannibalism of the following passage:

[1] *Two Phases of Criticism,* in the volume entitled *The Heart of Man and Others Papers,* by George E. Woodberry.

"The classic, the chivalric, the Christian world attest the fact, broadly; and in individual life how must we ourselves bear witness to the mingling in ourselves of the poet's blood—which is the blood of the world."

To some it may seem unjust, even knavish, to so ruthlessly assail the criticism of the venerable author of *The North Shore Watch,* but the inconsistencies are so patent, the diction so vague, the position so untenable, that no other method would suffice. Let us return, however, to the earlier portions of the essay, the discussion of historical criticism, where the Professor pursues a more lucid form of exposition, and note the lacunæ and errata. There is no definition of what historical criticism is supposed to embody, no stating of whether it is to be mere intimacy with battles, state decrees, to amours of royalty, the superficial descriptions of the customs and idiosyncrasies of a people, and no attempt to show how this historical criticism is the outgrowth of the social and economic forces active at the time. Moreover, though the author under consideration might not disagree, he never dares to state that the so-called esthetic criticism is built upon historical criticism, and is as helpless without its support as a fallen leaf before a gust. And, what is even more significant, there is not a single admission of the necessity of the historical, or, what would be more accurate, sociological, approach to modern as well as ancient and mediæval art. Sociological criticism of contemporary literature is as indispensable as sociological criticism of Greek drama, bourgeois tragedy of the eighteenth century, or the rise of romanticism in the nineteenth. Without knowledge of the social forces that have gone into its making, the object cannot be understood with anything like fullness, appreciation of its value must be decisively limited, and security of criticism rendered thin and precarious. "To see the object as in itself it really is," the aim of criticism according to Arnold, is impossible without knowledge of all the causes of its creation and character. The relation of a piece of art to its environment from which it has necessarily sprung is the fundamental means that we have of tracing and interpreting its birth and evolution. The object cannot be seen "as in itself it really is" if examination of its immediate features is made to preclude analysis of its social origin and growth.

Let us divert our attention from the work of Professor Woodberry to that of several of his competitors in the clash of American criticism. From the pseudo-esthetes, as Ernest Boyd has aptly described them, we have the muddy logic of voluntarism, coated with the frailties of diluted diction and the vaguenesses of mystical rhetoric:

"In the world where morals count we have failed to give them (the poets) the proper material out of which to rear a nobler edifice. Insofar as this is inherent in the nature of our humanity, *it is not affected by the special conditions of society in space and time.*" (Spingarn.)

This is ridiculously inexact criticism. Poets can no more remain unaffected "by the special conditions of their society" than can scientists or philosophers. Every individual, be he a maniac or genius, must get his ideas from his social environment, and to speak of his not being affected by this environment is sheer fatuity. This tendency to rhapsodize regardless of reality betrays one of the underlying weaknesses of our civilization. But the essential method of "the new critical theory" has yet to be examined—and assailed! Carlyle, closely paraphrasing if not exactly quoting the words of Goethe, was the second of the moderns to state this approach, which of recent years has been called the Spingarn-Croce-Carlyle-Goethe heory. What is the theory?

"What has the writer proposed to himself to do? And how far has he succeeded in carrying out his plan?"

This is one statement of it. It may be well to indicate another. The critic's first and foremost duty is to make plain to himself "what the poet's aim really and truly was, how the task he had to do stood before his eye, and how far, with such materials as were afforded him, he has fulfilled it."

Now we do not intend in this essay to attack the theory *per se,* which as an airy sort of definition is not without value although its implications are so numerous as to seriously narrow and obfuscate its meaning, but Spingarn's handling of it. Spingarn is its American propagandist. In American criticism, therefore, it is Spingarn and not Carlyle or Croce that is to be held accountable for its promotion. With this theory Spingarn believes he has discovered at last the relationship between morality and art—that there is none—and distinguishes pure esthetics, in the way of criticism, from science. He voices the ancient claim, so egregiously erroneous, "of the free and original movement of art," maintaining, like the idealist, in order to give his position the appearance of tenability, that art is the cause and not the effect of social evolution. The "hunting" art of the Bushmen, since all art, in accordance with his theory, expresses "free and original movement," would be the cause of their relegation to the hunting and fishing state of existence, at least one of the vitally determining factors, and not the result of this semi-barbarous stage of economic struggle. The critic seems to imagine that we paint before we eat, that men fought originally for art-expression and not for food. It was only when economic difficulties were lightened that art-creation could begin to grow. The history of primitive art provides irrefragable proof of this contention. It is consequently illogical to talk about "the free and original movement of art" when in reality the concepts and technique of art are dependent upon the movement of material conditions, the source of food-power, the drive of invention, the advance of social organization. Esthetic changes are but corollaries of the material. Furthermore, according to Spingarn, who in this instance is in decisive opposition to Professor Woodberry, historical (or sociological) criticism cannot be esthetic criticism because it shoots us off at a tangent, removing us further from the art object rather than bringing us closer to it:

"We have done with the race, the time, the environment of a poet's work as an element in criticism." [2]

If a critic avoid the sociological method, how is it possible for him to know "what the writer proposed to himself to do" . . . "what the poet's aim really and truly was," or "how the task he had to do stood before his eye, and how far, with such materials as were afforded him, he has fulfilled it"? One can only under-

[2] *The New Criticism,* Spingarn.

stand what the writer has "proposed to himself to do" when one knows the esthetic concepts, products of his contemporary sociology, that molded his work, and that imbued him with his art incentive. The poet's aim is no free and spontaneous thing, winging itself into the empyrean without the trammels of reality. After all, the very imagination of the poet is determined by the realities that confront him. Poets do not write of seraphim and cherubim now as they did in previous centuries when these traceries of religious fancy were accepted as parts of religious reality. Nor do they concern themselves, except in historical romance, with the intrigues and tribulations of court, though the vestiges of royalty still cling like somnambulistic phantoms to the edge of conservative society. The cry of the esthetes is the echo of the purblind idealist, groping wildly for a promise of freedom in a materially determined world. Their esthetic criticism, as a consequence, is fragmentary and inconclusive, as recklessly impressionistic as the impressionists they decry.

Professor Stuart Sherman reveals another attitude. His outlook is more astringent and puritanical, avowedly and audaciously so, than that of his rivals. The study of literature becomes a study in ethics for one of his mind. Nothing could more exactly express the opposite of his position than the following sentence of Spingarn:

"To say that poetry, as poetry, is moral or immoral, is as meaningless as to say that an equilateral triangle is moral and an isosceles triangle immoral."

Professor Sherman does not want to purify American literature of puritanism. Toward the moral laxity of the new trend in American literature he is sneeringly inimical. Placing himself among "the ordinary puritanical Americans" he declares that "beauty, whether we like it or not, has a heart full of service," and accuses contemporary art of pandering to "sensual gratification" and propagating the curiously related doctrine that "God cares nothing for the Ten Commandments or for the pure in heart," Professor Sherman's jeremiad does not soften into a plea as he continues to disentangle the threads of our national genius:

"It is certainly not by banishing or ignoring the austerer ministers and making poetry, painting, and music perform a Franko-Turkish dance of sensual invitation—it is not thus that the artist should expect to satisfy a heart as religious, as moral, and as democratic as the American heart is, by its bitterest critics, declared to be."

There is but little resiliency of judgment in a declaration of that nature. In fact it is a counterfeit aspersion. American literature presents no such picture. The modern generation is not clever enough to create a voluptuary utopia, vitiated by the absence of intellectual appeal. Its recent reaction toward sex is but the natural result of the supremacy of the fettering bourgeois ethics of the latter half of the eighteenth and first seventy-five years of the nineteenth centuries. Professor Sherman's alarm, then, is unwarranted and deserving of no better reward than ridicule.

But there are other places where the Professor stumbles accidentally on several half-truths. These even are rarely to be discovered in American criticism. Professor Sherman is more of a social critic than the others we have discussed. His social rationalizations, of course, are unfortunately tainted with didacticism. He seems to belong to the Mme. de Stael group in his belief that literature is, or at least should be, an expression of society, and argues with curious circumlocutoriness in defense of this thesis. His logic, however, is very weak and superficial. He says well, for instance, that "when a great artist expresses himself completely, it is found invariably that he has expressed, not merely himself, but also the dominant thought and feeling of the men with whom he lives," but then concludes, with ludicrous insensitivity to art-values and the influence of class-conflicting social factors upon literature, that Theodore Dreiser is an inferior artist because he does not express the traits of the American bourgeois class. The bourgeois class in America represent the essence and finesse of our culture for Professor Sherman; their prudery and pseudo-puritanism, their sectarian religiosity and vain affectation for the principles of democracy, are the characteristics of our "national genius." These traits, not seen as clearly as we have described them, arouse no indignation or complaint; in fact they are the embodiment of "profound moral idealism" for the critical Professor. Continuing in the same tenor Professor Sherman makes an observation that might have been pregnant with significance had it been more profound and complete.

"At any rate, if the great artist, in expressing himself, expresses also the society of which he is a part, it would seem to follow, like a conclusion in geometry, that a great American artist must express the *profound moral idealism* of America. To rail against it, to lead an insurrection against it, is to repeat the folly of the Restoration wits. If in this connection one may use a bit of the American language, it is to *buck* the national genius, and this is an enterprise comparable with bucking a stone wall."—(Italics mine.)

Professor Sherman's attitude, however inconsistent and laughably didactic, certainly is more engagingly and suggestively sociological than that of Spingarn or Woodberry or Brownell. Sherman sees that society has a deep influence on literature, but that no artist can escape this influence he does not perceive—or will not admit. Furthermore, his conception of society has about it something of the visionary unity of eighteenth-century metaphysics. It takes into account no divisions of class-psychology, no social trend other than the immediately ascendant. It is excruciatingly fixed and contorted, without the remotest evolutionary aspect. What is, is good because it is; that which opposes what is, is bad because it was good for the pioneer. Religion is good for us because it strengthened our forefathers —and inspired Arthur Sullivan to write "Onward Christian Soldiers." In the times of Abraham, Professor Sherman would have been hallelujahing for polygamy, the sixteenth century would have discovered him clamoring for the sacrifice of Bruno, the seventeenth for the annihilation of the theater. The attitude that would have been different in separate ages is static in its own.

What Professor Sherman should have seen but didn't is that Theodore Dreiser is not "bucking" the national genius or "bucking a stone wall," but "bucking" the bourgeois conception. He should realize that the bourgeois is one class in society, and that it is in active, intensive conflict with the proletarian. The very struggle of "capital and labor" should have given him disturbing evidence of this fact, but for the usual literary mind "capital and labor" is a problem too unesthetic to consider. That the pinnacle of bourgeois ethics and

[163]

esthetics may be shaken by the extravagant and irresponsible fatuities of a youthful generation is not to be doubted, but that it should ever topple is inconceivable to the intelligence of the unchanging superannuated mind. The impermanency of ethical and esthetic values should prove a permanent irritation to the conservative intellect—but it doesn't. This intellect is as subtle as the ostrich in its ratiocinations. That Dreiser represents a trend the decisive antithesis of the bourgeois is undeniable. Although Professor Sherman is cognizant of this fact, he entirely fails to see that it is precisely this proletarian trend which Dreiser represents that is rising, and the bourgeois trend, in its heyday with Thackeray, Longfellow, and Howells, and still in the temporary ascendant, that is steadily beginning to wane. To maintain that all artists who combat bourgeois predilections are anathema is consistent with Professor Sherman's philosophy, and he has the privilege of shallowly advocating their condemnation until the doom of his set, but to assert that these combatants are "bucking the national genius" is preposterously, unforgivably stupid. The national genius is not a crystallized conception, firmly grooved and susceptible to no oscillation. According to the Shermanian logic, W. D. Howells and H. W. Longfellow would be superior to Sherwood Anderson and Carl Sandburg, because the latter two "bucked" the national genius—the bourgeois concepts—and the former did not. "Bucking the national genius," which is equivalent to saying "bucking the esthetics of the reigning class," has been a sport that the literati have been deliciously guilty of for many centuries. Lillo, Lessing, Diderot, Zola, Whitman, all "bucked the national genius" in their respective countries—must they therefore be called inferior? Shall we consider Huxley inferior to Wilberforce because he "bucked" the national genius and the latter was not intelligent enough so to do, or Brandes inferior to Howells for the same reason? To be really confidential, Professor Sherman seems to be "bucking" himself—and not any too delicately.

THE VAUDEVILLE CRITIC, H. L. MENCKEN

CERTAINLY Mr. Mencken is unique. But so is a tight rope walker or a hobo. His influence is undoubtedly widespread and penetrating. He is the prophet of the tawdry run of anti-bourgeois liberals. But there is even a contradiction in Mr. Mencken's sentimentality. An anti-bourgeois in morals, he is a thorough bourgeois in economics. His philosophy, as we shall show, abounds in the social contradictions and solecisms of the puerile Nietzschean. Superficiality is his foremost attribute.

[165]

Yet Mr. Mencken is heralded as a famous man, perhaps America's most noteworthy contributor to the *science* of criticism. Myriads of readers peruse his writings with unfeigned gusto and admiration. Criticasters
write uncritical eulogies about his skill and profundity.
Muddled intellectuals refer to him as an authority.

Now let us remove Mr. Mencken for a moment from
his *Smart Set* Parnassus and examine his pretensions
to significance. What is Mr. Mencken's theory of
criticism? ⸱ Criticism for him is a creative art, as lively
a manifestation of the artistic genius as a tragedy or
lyric. "Criticism," he exclaims, as unanalytically as
usual, "is a fine art or nothing. Let us forget all the
heavy effort to make a science of it." Of this error in
logic many other critics are as guilty as Mr.
Mencken. Yet it is an entire misconception of the
purpose of criticism. It springs from a slippery evasion of definition. Art makes its primary and immediate appeal to the emotions, arousing feelingful rather
than intellectual reactions. The intellect is concerned
with the comparison of ideas, the measured analysis
and discrimination of causes and attributes, the at-
testing of values, the predictions of change. Although
these activities can be influenced by visceral variations,
they are none the less ideational and not emotional.
In writing a story we endeavor to awaken the emotions,
at the most to create a kind of intuitive appreciation

[166]

of life, and not to present a logical teleology, a sequential theory of numbers, or a mathematical synthesis of the sciences. It is in its approach and method, therefore, that art is different from science. Criticism, despite the Spingarnian and Menckenian protests to the contrary, is a science and not an art. By that we do not mean that it is an exact science such as physics, or that it has established any indubitable laws or generalizations, but that its method is that of a science and not of an art. The word criticism is derived originally from the Greek word *krinein,* meaning to judge or discern, and all judgment, however much of a rationalization in fundament, is an intellectual and not emotional procedure. In judgment we dissect, weigh and evaluate—an intellectual scientific act that is widely distinct from art creation. Situations in a novel, for example, are chosen not because they prove the logic of a theory or reduce the substance to its lowest common denominator, but because they give what the author believes to be the highest artistic effect. A great painter does not aim to catch "the moment" in order to prove intoxicants to be evil or social philosophies to be obsolescent, but to arouse an emotional reaction. The intellectual element in art is subordinated to the emotional. Literature, of course, is the most intellectual and logical of the arts, because it deals with words which represent ideas, but the use of words in literature, the drama, the novel, the short story, the lyrical essay, is different from their use in science or philosophy. In the former, words are used to awaken states of feeling; in the latter, states of knowing. This is a difference that can be neglected only by the sciolist. In fact, in the whole controversy regarding this issue Mr. Mencken contradicts himself, and affirms our point, when he says that "prose, however powerful its appeal to the emotions, is always based primarily upon logic, and is thus scientific"—an admission that criticism, since it is prose, is a science and not an art—just above, as we noted, he declared in reference to criticism, that we should "forget all the heavy effort to make a science of it; it is a fine art or nothing." Of course, his failure to distinguish types of prose and their sundry objects is painfully noticeable. But inconsistency is another of Mr. Mencken's important attributes. In one place he writes one thing, and in another scathingly ridicules it. In his essay on *The Novel,* he writes, in prophecy of the *great feminine novel* of 1950 that "it (the novel) will seem harsh, but it will be true. And being true, it will be a good novel. There can *be no good one that is not true,*" and then in his sentimental essay on *Foot Note on Criticism* he states that "what saved Carlyle, Macaulay and company is as plain as day. *They could make the thing charming, and that is always a*

million times more important than making it true."
(Italics mine.) Or if we want a still further contradiction of the latter declaration we can turn to Mr. Mencken's latest book, his essay captioned audaciously *Toward a Realistic Esthetic*:

"When a man speaks or believes an untruth he certainly makes no progress with his conquest of Nature. (Italics mine.) On the contrary, he plainly gives up the battle, at least for the moment. Instead of fighting resolutely and effectively, and so improving his state, he simply buries his head in the sand." Now what is of more value, the charming or the true? Throw up the dice!

When criticism attempts to become a "creative art" it stultifies its purpose—and fails to be criticism. It becomes an exercise in the emotions, a flaunting of pet idiosyncrasies and repressed desires, and, as with Mr. Mencken, resolves itself into a literary soliloquy racing *pari passu* with jazz. Our objection is not that such essays cannot be interesting, curious as revelations of personality, fascinating as examples of descriptive eloquence and subtlety of diction, but that they are not critical. Criticism consists of a different method, a different content. It essays to examine and compare, to calculate and judge. Its object is not primarily to entertain, to regale the reader with confessional ecstasies, flashes of fancy, or scraps of gossip,

[169]

but to dissect and evaluate. Its aim is not to create a work of art, but a work of analysis—of logic.

Yet Mr. Mencken considers himself a critic—not an *impolite* essayist, which is his exact function. It is true that he is critical of philosophy, politics, prohibition, and socialism. But is his "criticality" emotional or intellectual? Is there any indication that the things whereof he speaks are understood by him with anything resembling thoroughness? Let us see!

"The essential thing about democracy, as every one must know, is that it is a device for strengthening the have-nots in their eternal war upon the haves. That war, as every one knows again, has its psychological springs in envy pure and simple, envy of the more fortunate man's greater wealth, the superior pulchritude of his wife or wives, his larger mobility and freedom, his more protean capacity for and command of happiness—in brief, his better chance to lead a bearable life in this worst of possible worlds. It follows that under democracy, which gives a false power and importance to the have-nots by counting every one of them as the legal equal of George Washington or Beethoven, the process of government consists largely, and sometimes almost exclusively, of efforts to spoil that advantage artificially. Trust-busting, free silver, direct elections, prohibition, government ownership and all the other varieties of American political quackery are but symptoms of the same general rage."

To simulate Mr. Mencken for a moment, this is bombastic balderdash. Is there any apprehension of economic change or social evolution in this rampant race of phrase, this indiscriminate explosion of sentiment? Is there any appreciation of the social forces that have created this "rage" of democracy, and understanding of why "trust busting, free silver, direct elections, government ownership" are expressive of a comparatively recent development of the capitalist system and not of its earlier career? Mr. Mencken objects to the "false power and importance (given) to the have-nots by counting every one of them as the legal equal of George Washington or Beethoven," yet would he have objected to the counting of Poe, Stephen Crane, and Walt Whitman because they were assuredly "have-nots"? Yet the distinction of haves and have-nots is unmistakably economic. According to Menckenian sagacity, there is no difference between the proletarian of this century and the serf of the Middle Ages, except that the latter was more pleasant because he worried his superiors with less frequency. The socialization of labor under capitalism seems to indicate nothing of importance for Mr. Mencken; it signifies no difference in social evolution, no difference in ideas from the individualism of labor during the eighteenth and early nineteenth centuries.

[171]

Let us take another example of Menckenian perspicacity and profundity. An eminently powerful conclusion:

"Socialism indeed is simply the degenerate capitalism of bankrupt capitalists."

It is difficult to refute such austere logic. Or to refer to Mr. Mencken's debate with LaMonte is but to introduce the reader to another piece of no less inspiring sequence of argument. How ridiculous have been the various criticisms of socialist theory, the long extended studies of the materialist conception of history, the analyses of class struggle, the dissection of Marxian economics, when Mr. Mencken has been able to despatch the matter in the pithy brevity of a sentence. Had only these critics known of Mr. Mencken's contribution they could have omitted their studies and avoided their discussions. Another chronological misfortune, to be sure.

Prohibition! It is here that Mr. Mencken soars on the wooden wings of a poetaster. All of the erudition and wisdom of a philosopher are brought to the fore in the ethical concerto, captioned *The Dry Millennium*. Prohibition is seen to have profound effects upon the population problem, marriage, idealism, and the instinct to sadism. Rustic adolescents will no

longer invade the cities in hordes, car-conductor service
will suffer as a consequence, and bordello-traffic be
minus some of its clowns; bachelors will be driven to
marriage because of the intolerable aridity of an unin-
toxicated life; the sensation of persecution, aggravated
by innumerable raids and sundry infringements upon
personal liberty, will become a national craving on the
part of the puritan, and American civilization will become as unpalpitating and colorless as that of Holland.
The working man alone will remain comparatively unaffected. He will accept the new state of affairs as inevitable, gradually acquiesce as to its wisdom, and thus
solemnly goose-step with the rest of the puritans. Now
one must admit that this is a marvelous panoramic survey of contemporary America which is so gravely afflicted with the Prohibition plague. It is true that Mr.
Mencken does not discuss the economic significance
of Prohibition, or the origin of the puritanic temper
which has projected this onslaught on "drink," or manifest any intimacy with the social forces that have
brought about the peculiar psychology of the "puritan prohibitionist"—but, after all, such analysis is
scarcely necessary for the vaudeville critic who has but
the superficial Nietzscheans of the twentieth century
to entertain.

In this criticism of Mr. Mencken's criticism, however, we do not want to be misunderstood. Although we do not esteem Mr. Mencken as a critic in the real sense of the word, as we illustrated in the earlier part of the essay, we do not consider his works to be without interest or appeal. An impressionist in method he has diverged from the impressionist style in that he has substituted breeziness for brilliance, piquancy for pathos, and startling colloquialisms for startling imagery. He is a vaudevillian, not an analyst. To employ the phrase of an English critic, his "heavenly messenger appears in pink tights." [1] This calls to mind the words of Ben Hecht:

"Mencken is what you might call a healthy force. His attacks on our brahmins are delightful. Of course, he is no judge of literature. His approval means less than that of any critic in America—it means simply that you have good literary manners. Mencken is unable to fix the type of artist he examines. He is America's soapbox orator, street corner shouter and table thumper. He has no feeling for moods, rhythm or style."

He writes to amaze and startle, to provide a feast of wild and rushing conclusions, hastily digested, and not to select, classify, and judge. Very often we do not disagree with his conclusions, while we do disagree

[1] *The Criterion,* Foreign Review Section. Page 152, Vol. III, No. 9.

vigorously with the way he arrives at them. His championings of Conrad and Dreiser, his praise of *Ethan Frome, My Antonia,* and *Old Wives' Tale,* his appreciation of Whitman, Crane, and Hardy, to set together an odd trio, arouse nothing but agreement, but do these enthusiasms command attention because of the discriminating logic and analysis which characterizes their pronouncement or because of the peculiar Menckenian vulgarities and crude witticisms in which they are clothed? Unable to use a chisel, Mr. Mencken employs a bludgeon.

In what might be termed purely literary criticism, Mr. Mencken at least is less ill-adept than in his more general strictures, his concern with politics and economics, prohibition and feminism. For a single illustration let us take his essay on Conrad which has earned him no little esteem. It would be folly to say that this essay is without interest, the same as it would be folly to say that it is significant criticism. Now what does Mr. Mencken say in this essay? First, that Conrad's work is permeated with a kind of masculine melancholy—there is nothing weak or feminine about the melancholy of this brooding Pole—free from mystical evasion or spiritistic fancy, a melancholy that is "forever fascinated by the immense indifference of things, the tragic vanity of the blind groping that we

[175]

call aspiration, the profound meaninglessness of life."
Like Ibsen, Conrad offers no solutions. His writing
is pure of doctrine or dogma, unruffled by gusts of
circumstance or vicissitudes of evolution. He is a
cosmic artist. The trivialities of sex, the problems of
virtue, the thready tissues of sentimentality are elements comparatively foreign to his work. His characters show "ineluctably vivid and persuasive personality," his descriptions challenge "the pictorial vigor
of Hugo and the esthetic sensitiveness of Lafcadio
Hearn and surpass them both," his situations, plot-in-
volvements and sequences of motive possess "indubitable veracity." And, of course, there is notice
of the price of Conrad's first editions, of the failure of
Victory as a "magazine novel," of the faint-hearted re-
ception of *Almayer's Folly,* and comments on Anglo-
Saxon quackery and pyrotechnics.

In an analysis of such an essay the first feature to
be noted is its lack of analysis. Is there any dissection of the novels discussed, any attempt to indicate by
cogent comparisons their strength and weakness, any
endeavor to evaluate by means of dimensioned co-
ordinates the respective scenes and characters involved? A few fluttering phrases of condemnation—
The Return is a thoroughly infirm piece of writing, a
second rate magazine story . . . *The Inheritors* is

[176]

worse, it becomes, after the first few pages, a flaccid artificiality, a bore—with splashes of commendatory descriptives, interspersed between discussions of the influence of the sea and the impotency of human striving, is all that can be discovered. Now these things are interesting but obvious, striking but surfacy. Their detection reveals no singular acuity of vision or extraordinary brilliance of interpretation. Arthur Symons caught the same sentiment and projected it with emotion-provoking vividness in his essay on Conrad, an adventure in impressionistic art, not criticism. Although dissimilar in style, Wilson Follett's appreciation of the Conradian metaphysic was not dissimilar in content. These criticisms, all of them, lack historical perspective and philosophic inclusiveness, however. Important or great criticism, as Henry James aptly declared, "seems to us to touch more or less nearly on pure philosophy"; the great critic, to continue to quote from James, "is a compromise between a philosopher and a historian," and his task is "to compare a work with itself, with its own concrete standard of truth." [2] Mr. Mencken's method is torturingly narrow. It is content to deal with the patent. For the sake of a witticism it will sacrifice a truth. Evolution in literature is not a member of its glittering gallery of esthetic

[2] *Notes and Reviews: A French Critic.* By Henry James.

conceptions. In studying Conrad it makes no analysis of racial and social consciousness, takes into account no influence of social environment, but considers the artist as an object apart, an undetached phenomenon swinging upon a self-erected pivot. This is the fallacy of what is often called "pure criticism." It fails to see the relationship of art to life, the determining factors that create and shape artistic tendencies and expression. It is unconcerned with the reasons why Conrad has written a different type of sea-story from Marryat, or why the sea today has a different meaning and effect than it had in the days of Scott. It does not even possess the biographical lucidity of second-rate criticism. It approaches reality as if the latter were a fixed entity, capable of being understood solely in terms of its present form without knowledge of the intertwining tracery of causes that have given it shape and made it an esthetic necessity. In brief it is squinty profile criticism—if it must be called criticism.

Yet Mr. Mencken is representative of our present generation. He is representative of an era that precedes collapse. His verbal antics and inconsistencies of logic vividly reflect the chaotic indecision and contradiction of our time—and nation. Our mind is still afflicted with dubiety and myopia. It revolts against bourgeois ethics, but not against bourgeois economics.

It is feverish and frenetic, insurrectionary of mood, but without knowledge of direction. It is content with superficial remonstrance. It realizes deficiencies but prefers to laugh at them—not to lessen or eliminate them. And so Mr. Mencken thrives!

MORALS AND DETERMINISM

ALL the philosophic arguments of the ages can be reduced to a simple basis of difference. This division of attitude has reflected itself in many ramified paths of thought, in a diversity of material too extensive to describe, and yet, beneath all the mass of bewildering and reckless terminology, beneath the obscurantism of medieval metaphysicians, the entelechies of contemporary biologists, and the generalizations of modern science, the division can be seen and traced. It is an attitude toward life, toward the world and the universe, that marks the division. Two decisively different types of mind represent each attitude. The differing attitudes revolve about the question of man's nature. Is it determined or free?—this is the basis of difference. Is the activity of man as determined as the activity of matter? Are the human body and mind forced to behave in definite ways, according to their structure and environment, in the same fashion that we observe the motion and change of matter, or do they possess a distinguishing freedom of their own? Does the multiplicity of human response prove its capacity for freedom of choice? Is society fundamentally a result of individual wishes or of the objective laws of production? [1] Are our ideas determined by environment, or do they have a quality of the transcendental in their substance? The one type of mind discriminately and without disquietude can view human reaction as determined, basically reflex, the other cannot. The one type craves for a secret essence, an *élan vital,* a certain disembodied force that gives to protoplasm a peculiar freedom from causality; the other does not. The one so desires man's freedom and all of the power and supremacy that seem to go with it, that it will rationalize rather than admit the facts that confront it; the other will not. The one bases itself upon the laws of logic and physics, the other upon the laws of the spirit. The one type, the voluntarist, is utopian, the other type, the determinist, is scientific.

In every philosophic controversy the two types conflict. In science, notwithstanding its empirical character, a remnant of the voluntarist ideology is perpet-

[1] It is interesting to note here that the belief that the body acts in any other than mechanical ways is no longer tenable in modern medicine, and yet, notwithstanding the empirical data establishing it, a refutation of the attitude still exists in the Christian Science movement. Prayer, of course, in every religion, is viewed in a somewhat similar mystic light. It is well to observe that where the majority now admit the mechanical nature of the operations of the body, they still insist upon believing in the old separationist hypothesis, that the mind is something that acts independently of the body, and therefore is free. The mere rudiments of physiology expose the fallacy of such a belief. Reduced to a figure, it is like a bird with snapped wings struggling to fly in a cyclonic storm gust.

[181]

uated in the vitalist movement. Also a few of the Dana-ist evolutionists still cling to the utopian attitude. In historical theory we have the materialist conception of Marx and Engels, and the romantic conception of Guizot [2] and Carlyle. In psychology today there is the same conflict between the determinist and voluntarist schools as there was between the theories of Taine and Guyau. The differences between Dreisch and Loeb are elementally the same as those between Bergson and Taine. The one type believes in a strange and fleeting creative evolution, in an autonomy of impulse, the other in a natural and definite because necessitarian evolution, with impulse but an inevitable reflection of the myriad transformations of this process. In physiology the Johannes Müller school prevailed at least until the middle of the nineteenth century and only gradually has been supplanted by the mechanist, which has attempted to reduce physiological reaction to a physical and chemical basis. In epistemology the dispute between the idealist and materialist can be re-

[2] Guizot, it should be remembered, however, at moments did pierce deeper into the moving causes of history than is usually thought, although the coordination of his facts was seldom profound or complete. In his essays, for instance, he often committed himself to a halfway materialist position. The following sentences of his are quoted as an example: "In order to understand political institutions, it is necessary to study the different castes that exist within a given society, and their mutual relations. To understand these different social castes we must know the nature of their property (land) relations."—Guizot, *Essays,* pp. 73, 74. Dixieme Edition, 1880.

solved into the same division of attitude; the idealist shifts his knowledge, and means of getting it, to a vague and undetermined concept that the most searching investigation can neither attack nor solve, the materialist founds his upon practical data, limited by the environment and constitutional susceptibility of the mind. William James, who sensed this difference in a rather obscure and nebulous fashion, speculatively remarked that it might be due entirely to differences in the liver. A more thorough analysis, however, would show that whatever organic change may take place, and act as the direct cause of the attitude of mind of the individual, the underlying and driving cause is the environment. Eccentricities in the liver do not occur without an environmental cause of some kind, nor do eccentricities in the nature or activity of any other organ or cell. Although environment may not be the immediate cause, it nevertheless is the fundamental one, for any predispositions to nephritic, hepatic, or any other disease transmitted through the germ-plasm had to get their initial cause from the environment in order that the germ-plasm might be so affected. Put in other terms, heredity, which is to be traced to the germ-plasm and which is noted in the character of predisposition, can have no other origin than environment, and, fundamentally speaking, can be modified

[183]

only by environmental influences. James spoke of the tender and tough-minded types in illustration of this difference. It would have been more accurate and profound to use the attributes tender and tough in reference to environment; the soft and coddling environment of the bourgeois being described as tender, and the rugged and astringent environment of the proletarian being characterized as tough. And yet from both of these respective environments, broadly speaking, arise divergent and contrasting types. Environment described in the wide classifications of bourgeois and proletarian, then, is not alone sufficient to account for the division of attitude with which we are concerned in this discussion, and it becomes necessary to recognize the potency of numerous subtle stimuli that the environment affords, in order to understand with perfect clarity all the changes that often bring about the disparities of outlook that we have described. In the period immediately following, sometimes before, birth and during early childhood and puberty, for instance, we can discover many environmental stimuli that bring with them not only narcissistic and schizophrenic reactions, but also the propelling motives toward optimism and pessimism, tenderness and toughness. It is not the psychological statement, then, that the disparity is entirely due to a difference of visceral 'response, with which we quarrel, but with the fact that the statement fails to appreciate that the difference of visceral response is originally and essentially a matter of environmental influence. A new and more scientifically constructed environment, therefore, must bring about eventually, if not immediately, a change in visceral response, and it is certainly not hazardous to predict that the cry for utopian conceptions will diminish as the environment and the individual become more harmoniously adjusted to each other. And with this adjustment will arise the undisputed supremacy of science and of the scientific, the determinist, or the tough, attitude.

The peculiar expressions that these attitudes of mind have taken in respective periods of history have been determined always by the conditions of the times, telluric and social. While the telluric conditions which are primary in origin, and in that sense the determinants of the social, are of a comparatively static character in that they do not change in any marked way [4] from age to age, the social conditions are in a constant process of evolution. The morals of a people, therefore, as was indicated in an early part of this article, however telluric in origin, are immediately a result of

[4] Of course, from a geological point of view, they are in an incessant state of flux, but insofar as their effect upon man is concerned, they do not vary in any perceptible fashion.

the altering rotations of social change. Social change, in its wide aspects, is brought about by change in the means of production. Change in the means of production comes as a result of discovery and invention, themselves the products of a necessity created by the extant method of life. Man's morals changed as he emerged from the hunting and fishing stage into that of the pastoral because his ideas changed, and morals are nothing more than the reflection of the ideas that a society holds toward the world and man. Likewise the domestication of plants, subsequent to the domestication of animals, which meant the advent of the agricultural stage, caused another change in ideas and morals, and again with the introduction of machinery and the growth of industrialism came the evolution of a still different and newer ethic. All of these changes in methods of production followed *inevitably* from the development and decline of the various systems from which they sprang, and so did the morals which each system represented, but the problem of their advantages and disadvantages, values and disvalues, is not, therefore, in any way solved.

It is one thing to say that a system of morals, or a system of production, has been determined in its minutest particulars by the environment and has been inevitable, and quite another to give it an evaluation in satisfactory and precise terms. Although we can say with certainty that in the course of historical events, with the increasing concentration of capital and the steady organization and growing class consciousness of the working class, socialism is inevitable, we cannot say with equal certainty that socialism will be good or bad. The existence of capitalism was inevitable; a necessary stage in economic evolution, and without which socialism, in a scientific sense, could never develop, and yet the matter as to whether capitalism is, or was, good or bad still remains a controversial issue. For some capitalism has been good; for others, surely the majority, it has been bad. In the sense that capitalism was necessary for the development of industry, however,[5] and this in turn for the coming of socialism,[6] it was good; in the sense that it enslaved and tortured millions, and continues the process, it was and is bad. Rainfall is inevitable, but it may be good or bad according to the situation. It may be good for a farmer, but bad for a statesman who catches a cold from it and

[5] Without capitalism with its industrial characteristics, modern cities with their facilities for education, transportation, and increased production would not have been possible, and the only thing possible in the way of economic change would have been a kind of primitive, unprogressive communism, such as was found among the Indians and can be found today among some of the agricultural communities in Europe. What the Occident knows as progress, and education is included here, could never have come under such conditions.

[6] See *The Meaning of the Agricultural Tax*, by N. Lenin.

dies, and bad, likewise, for the country since he might have died at just a time when his influence was most needed in a great movement. Potassium cyanide solution, if drunk, we say is bad, and yet to the man who wants to die it is good. This conflict has been called the law of contradiction, and from it the assumption that truth is contradictory has been drawn. This is incorrect. It might be called, with far less qualm and debate, the law of moral or ethical contradiction. The terms good and true, throughout philosophical disputes, have been so intertwined and confused that as a result we now have a whole philosophy which is based upon the false union of the good and the true. *The good and the true are separate attributes and do not follow from every proposition.* It is a poetic desire, of course, to believe that whatever is true is good, and dreamful and illusory philosophies have been devoted to the justification of this belief. Truth is concerned with the correspondence between the mental picture of an object and the object itself, between idea and reality, whether ugly or beautiful, good or bad. The accuracy of a truth is to be determined by the accuracy of this correspondence. A thing may be true and yet evil. A diagnosis of cancer may be true and yet the effects of the truth upon the individual be harmful. That rainfall is caused by certain definite changes in the atmosphere, that it falls at a certain velocity, that it continues for a certain length of time and reaches a depth of a certain number of inches or a fraction of an inch, that it drenches and freshens the soil if it has been parched, that it brings disease to a statesman or washes a baby into a sewer, are truths, notwithstanding whom they please or pain. Truth is not happiness. Things are not true because they bring contentment to an individual; they may be methods towards a good adjustment, nothing more. It may be means of comfort and happiness, of unfrictional adjustment, for an aged woman, who has been reared in a religious environment, to believe in the immaculate conception and resurrection of Christ, but that does not mean that it is a truth. Untruths can often bring successful adjustments. A failing patient when told that he was growing stronger, to the doctor's surprise, has often recovered. Truth is not a method to gain pleasant results, or "an emotional belief which gives personal satisfaction." Good, interpreted in terms of harmonious adjustment, as was instanced in the case of the failing patient, may often come from an untruth. This distinction between the true and the good is of great importance. The trend of late American philosophy has shown that not only utopians and idealists fail to make this distinction. Truth is concerned with agreement between idea and reality, good with that which brings felicitous adjustment between the individual or individuals and environment.

But what is good and what is bad? This we have yet to determine. Are there any absolutes to settle this question? Are there any coördinates from which we can accurately judge? Although there is no law of contradiction in the matter of truth, there is contradiction in the matter of ethics. Whether this contradiction is ineradicable is something we must discover. We can begin with a broad proposition. Is life a good and death an evil? At first glance this might seem a simple and cogent division. But is it? To the suicide life must be an evil and death a good, or at least less of an evil than life. But the man who commits suicide is temporarily insane is one reply, and, the act itself is condemned by the others in the community is another. The insanity of the man, or the condemnation of his act, however, are not reasons to prove that live was not an evil to him and death a good. But the act was an evil to the community. Here we approach another phase. But how can such an act be an evil to a community? Can it be because it might inspire the community in the fashion that Hegesias' arguments did the Greeks? Or because the Schopenhauerian will to live is not released by self-annihilation?

Hardly! If we discover that the attitude of the community has been formed by the economic consequences that too frequently follow a suicide, the possible burial of the body at public expense, the burden of impoverished kin, the escape from responsibility for crime, is our problem any more satisfactorily clarified? Does the community believe death is an evil because it condemns self-motived death? Surely it has hospitals and physicians to ward off death, and certainly it does not want to ward off that which is good. Yet it has religions that endeavor to exalt death into a kind of transitional ecstasy, and metaphysics that give it a strange and haunting glamor. And, further, death when it takes the form of sacrifice for a noble cause becomes a good, not an evil. Can we say then that life, in the face of these numerous opposites, is a good, and death an evil?

Let us consider the problem of good more concretely and definitely. First of all there are two kinds of goods, individual and social. Anything that brings an individual into harmonious adjustment with his environment is a good, and, if we are to erect a hierarchy of *goods*, that which brings the individual into the most harmonious—and that means actively efficient—adjustment is the highest good, or series of goods, for him. But what is a social good? That which brings a community into an harmonious adjustment with its environment? And what is *harmonious* in both of these cases? Harmonious can only be used to describe that state of existence in which the reactions of the organism are pleasant, rather than painful, positive rather than negative, or, to put it in terms of energy, where the anabolic processes are in correct ratio with the katabolic. The criteria here are certainly far from positive or final. The coördinates that we establish in order to make our judgments must be entirely empirical, without the least quality of the utopian in their character. The degree to which man can harmoniously adapt himself to an environment, his full efficiency being utilized, must be determined. In individual *goods* there will be wide conflict, but there will also be certain basic agreements. Good food, good lodging, good clothes, and the like are *goods* mutually desired by all, and what *good* is, in such matters as food, lodging and clothes, must be settled by reference to some accepted norm. Now to turn to the social good, let us raise a question. Is a social good that which is good for all in the community? It can be, but that is very rarely the case. If it were, it would assume that the community in all cases was of the same kind, and each member in it could adjust himself with equal efficiency to a common situation. This, of course, is not scientifically true. A social good, ordinarily considered, is that which is good for the majority in the community. It may be good for one man to sit up in the early hours of the morning and sing and dance like a Corybantian, but bad for the rest of the community, who do not wish to have their slumber disturbed by his boisterous antics, and since this one man is a distinct minority it is necessary for him to forego what to him is an individual good for the sake of a social good. It is only the anarchist who would justify the man's action, the opinion of the majority notwithstanding. The philosophy of anarchism is based upon minority prerogative. But anarchism, as society is now constructed, would mean no government at all, or a myriad minorities, each representing conflicting and hostile governments. It would result in a decentralization that is in entire disconsonance with the trend of contemporary social evolution. Individual goods of necessity, then, when they come into conflict with social goods, must be sacrificed.

It seems inevitable, therefore, in determining a social good, that we retreat to the majority criterion. The will of the majority approaches closer to the general will and to the general happiness than the will of the minority. It is necessary to apply the mathematics of numbers, of course, in making such a judgment. Naturally there are many objections to this standard. Can we condemn the civilization of Athens, with its spurious democracy, but significant and influential art and metaphysics, because it prospered and developed through the efforts of its enslaved colonists? Had the enslavement of the colonists never taken place and they, the majority, been given the greater chance for freedom and happiness, could the Periclean age have flourished? Did the productive character of Greece at the time make slavery a necessity for social progress? The fact that slavery was inevitable at that time, and that it was necessary to the development of productive forces, which is an answer to the question, does not deny that when conditions exist which can permit the untrammeled expression of the best energies of men, the greater the number of effectual beings, the finer and greater the social result. Democracy of opinion, which is based on the majority—and socialism is but an extended development of this tendency—depends upon the material conditions to give it social validity. Although the American Indians with their primitive communism attained a measure of social contentment impossible under a regime of slavery or capitalism, they would have advanced in knowledge and art far beyond the state they did had the conditions driven them to slavery and later, through inventions, to capitalism. In an historical sense, then, we cannot say that the will of the majority in all of man's history functioned, or could have functioned, for his highest social good. In each of the periods, however, disregarding social advance from primitivism to socialism, the will of the majority at the time would have brought more happiness to the greater number—but not social progress. It is only when the majority become class-conscious, commonly certain of their aim, with their union in accord with the law of social evolution, that their will can serve as the best determinant of social good. The capacity of the majority to act in this fashion has only developed with their growing class-consciousness, which in turn has been fostered by the industrial system to which they have been enslaved. In view of the course of economic development, and also of the immediacy of the present situation, it is a necessity now that the matter of social good be decided by the happiness that it affords the greatest number.

But is the question finally solved? Is the majority to be considered as an immediate or historical entity? Shall man's immediate happiness be of more moment than the progress of the race? Shall the happiness of a temporary state of society be rated higher than the historical progress of the species which in its later evolution, however painful the present, will result in a more extensive and enduring felicity? We talk so easily and confidently of the value of majority decisions, without the least historical perspective. We answer the question that was raised before, as to the *good* of death when it is a sacrifice to a noble cause, by saying that

[195]

the death was only a good because it brought a greater good to the majority. If the man had died for an ignoble cause his death would not have been praised or the death classified as a good, because it would not have brought greater good to the majority. If we say that capitalism was an historical good at one time because it was necessary for the advent of socialism, we do not therefore say that it was a good for the existing millions who had to suffer under it, but was a good for the countless trillions who, in the future, will be able to thrive under a state of socialism which would not have been possible without this capitalism. Let us present an even more interesting example, quite aside from previous events, of the fallacy of the usual majority conception. The world at the present time has a human population of approximately one billion, seven hundred millions (1,700,000,000). Now suppose the earth should suffer another glacial invasion of far more gigantic and sweeping character than any of the numerous ones that occurred during the Pleistocene, indeed one of such severity that over seven-eighths of this total population should be exterminated, and yet out of this invasion, after its ravages had culminated and subsided, a super-race of men should emerge, would it be called good or bad? According to the majority of us living today, or at whatever time such an invasion took place, it would be an indubitable evil, and according to the ordinary majority concept it would be bad. Yet, in historical or anthropological description, man's development being viewed as an objective phenomenon, it would be an indubitable good. A social good, then, considered in historical perspective, does not necessarily have to be that which favors the majority at the existing moment—the majority in an æon rather than a generation being the shibboleth—but that which favors man as an objective unit in his struggle through the ages.[7]

When we scientifically adopt the conclusion at the present time that *it is a necessity that the matter of social good be decided by the happiness it affords the greatest number,* that the majority should be given the privilege of command, what we declare is that in accord with the law of social evolution the majority now is the unit capable of determining not only the good of the majority of today, but also of the coming centuries. We maintain in this that the growth and centralization of capital is steadily driving the workers into a state of class-consciousness, and in the process so educating them as to the origin and intensification of production that when the majority do become intelligently class-conscious they will be able to assume the control of

[7] Those who do not see how the successive systems of the past have served as the necessary predecessors of socialism, and in that sense the systems, with all of their tortuousness, must be considered as historical goods, should acquaint themselves with the full details of the materialist conception of history.

industry without serious rupture in its organization. And the workers being the majority, an ever-increasing majority, it should be noted, as capitalism continues to centralize, the decision will be a majority one. Of course, a sudden and unforeseen telluric calamity, as was suggested in the preceding paragraph, might shatter this conclusion as to social evolution, but since such events, as man's knowledge has gone, belong in the class of unaccountables, or incalculables, they have to be eliminated from our analysis.[8]

Throughout the previous discussion we have seen that the nature of society, its state of production and distribution, its political and religious ideas, its scientific and moral conceptions, have all been determined indirectly by the telluric and directly by the economic environment. We have seen further, in earlier sections of the article, that not only the activities of society are thus determined, but likewise those of the individual. Determinism of the social and economic kind is unsatisfactory and incomplete if it is not extended to include every activity of the individual. We have shown also that 'the only scientific attitude to take toward socialism is that it is inevitable, that it is in accord with the law of social evolution. The attitude which main-

[8] That does not mean that they are impossible—in fact the whole history of the earth has shown how very impending and existent they have been—or does it in any way invalidate the truth or importance of the illustration.

tains solely that socialism should come because it is fair and honest, because it is right and beautiful, because it will bring justice and equity to prevail among men, is the moral attitude of the utopian and is to be disapproved. Moral contradictions, as we have seen, too frequently obscure and confuse the issue. If capitalism has not reached a point of concentration where it is necessary to give way to another system of production and distribution, which implies that the workers are not in a sufficiently intelligent state of class-consciousness, any sudden revolution to bring about that change must finally result in a failure—moral justifications notwithstanding. In making our judgments in the context that capitalism and the systems that preceded it were historical goods because they were necessary in order that socialism could come into being, we necessarily made the consequent judgment that socialism will be a good, not because it is fair and honest, or because of any poetic land argument, but because it *means that with its coming the economic evolution of society will have reached such a stage where the majority will have become the scientific determinant of social good, and from which it follows that happiness, or actively efficient, harmonious adjustment, will come to the greatest number. This correlation between the ascent of the majority, in its capacity to become the determinant of social good, and the development of*

[199]

productive forces, is one of the most significant facts in the history of ethics and science.

The immediate problems of ethics, however, have yet to be considered. How does determinism affect man's moral concepts? Is his attitude toward his fellow-men changed with his acceptance of determinism? If the idea of personal responsibility is repudiated, will we not face a social chaos? Does the realization that all action, good or bad, is inevitable, alter the temper of his judgment?

Before answering these questions we shall first have to survey briefly the present attitude toward crime which in the eyes of conservative sociologists is our one social evil of cancerous character.

The legal systems of the world, with their minute forms of judicial procedure and strange and torturing methods of punishment, are uniformly based on the voluntarist hypothesis that all men are equally free to choose between good and evil. In the matter of crime punitive methods are resorted to for two reasons: First, as a means of protection to society, and secondly, as a form of social vengeance. Their use as a way to protection, however ineffectual, is commonly known and need not be further indicated at this point; as a means of social vengeance we have the horrendous examples of Southern lynchings, man-hunting expeditions for causes of rape and murder, and our own simple and barbarous "eye for eye, tooth for tooth" method of hanging or electrocution.   That these latter methods are not necessary for protection, every criminologist will maintain;[9] in fact they are but pure and unmistakable vestiges of the ancient savage cry of blood for blood.   That they have value in setting examples to inspire fear in the minds of the populace, particularly those with a propensity to criminality, is a deduction made from inclusive evidence.   It is part of that sciolistic sociology that is content to study effect without relation to cause, administer therapeutics without discovering the disease, and foster that dangerously illusive idea that fear will check crime.   Aside from the mere logic of the proposition, historical evidence has furnished abundant illustrations to show the absurdity of the idea.   A quotation from Fishman's *Crucibles of Crimes* is singularly appropriate:

"Years ago, in England, they hanged men for a large number of crimes, among them pocket picking.   Executions were public and many thousands of people attended them.   It was found that so many hundreds of persons engaged in picking the pockets of those who attended hangings for pocket pickings that the authorities were forced to abandon public executions.   When

[9] Life imprisonment, under proper supervision, is just as safe a protection as execution—only more costly to the state.

men pickpockets while watching others being hanged for the same offense, what little real deterrent effect punishment has can easily be seen."

Throughout the seventeenth and eighteenth centuries extremely stringent laws were passed in England to prevent the rising prevalence of criminality. Similar tactics were employed in Spain, France, and Italy, indeed, in every country in Europe. In England, for instance, during the eighteenth century, capital punishment was employed as the legal shift. Over a hundred criminal acts were made punishable by death, including such minor offenses as shoplifting, pocketpicking and illegal slaying of deer. We have seen by the above illustration the effect of the law upon pickpockets. The effect upon other criminals was not dissimilar. The statistics of the time show that crimes instead of decreasing actually became more numerous. Shoplifting instead of ceasing became a more practiced and shrewd art, and petty thefts of other character in no instance suffered diminution. Later Parliament repealed most of these laws and discovered that an outbreak of license did not occur, as the conservatives had scoldingly argued. The abolition of the debtor's prison, for instance, and the removal of penalty for debt, caused no increase in the number of debtors or

defaulted contracts.[10]   Darrow, in referring to the statistics, states "that the English people strangely found
out that so fast as they did away with punishing men
by death, crime decreased instead of increased; that
the smaller the penalty the fewer the crimes."   Such
a statement, however, is made in too hasty and unscientific a fashion.   The decrease in crimes that Darrow
noted did not result from the decrease in severity of
punishment, any more than an increase in crimes will
result from an increase in severity of punishment, but
from changes in the material conditions of the populace.   It should be mentioned also that the psychology
of the criminal is an exceptionally interwoven and complex affair.   His attitude toward the matter of penalty
is quite a contrast to what is usually imagined.   The
fact that hundreds of others have been caught and pun-
ished for the same offense that is to be perpetuated
again is not a deterrent to a mind driven by its environment to the verge of crime.   "Although others have
been caught, I shall escape" is an approximation of the
reasoning of the criminal in the premeditation of his
act; "they did not plan carefully enough, I shall; their

[10] In this same reference it is important to turn to Italy, where
Ferri reports that "the sole crime that has actually decreased in late
years is murder, for which punishment of death was abolished by law
in 1890."   Also Lombroso shows, by statistical proof, that in Italy
assaults were renewed and multiplied, notwithstanding the most
severe penalties, and also that as to brigandage, severity of punishment served only to increase it.   *L'unomo Delinquente,* 5th Edition,
Vol. III, pp. 8, 20.

weak points I shall strengthen; where they failed, I
shall succeed." It is precisely this kind of rationalization that the criminal mind is driven to, and lives by,
through stress of environment.

Buckle quite clearly showed by means of his collected facts and statistics that the number of criminals
increases just as the price of food soars. To introduce
the telluric factor more directly, Ferri has proven that
crimes against property show sudden increases in years
of severe winter, and "corresponding decreases in years
when the temperature is milder." Ferri has done more
thorough analysis and research into the nature and
history of crime than any other contemporary criminologist and his conclusion is significant to observe:

"This correspondence between the most general,
powerful and variable of the physical and social factors
of crime and the most characteristic manifestations of
crime, such as robberies, assaults and rapes, is so close
and constant that in my researches on criminality in
France, covering fifty years, whenever I found some
exceptional oscillation in these derelicts, I foresaw at
once that in the history of the same year there would
be, for example, an agricultural or financial crisis or a
political revolution, and in the meteorological statistics
a colder winter, a hotter summer, and the like. With
nothing but the plain line of a diagram of criminal
statistics, I was able to construct in their most salient

traits the historical vicissitudes of a whole country, thus confirming the actuality of these laws of criminal saturation by psychological experiment."[11]

Remedy for criminality, then, is not to be sought for in reprehensive measures of punishment, but in changes in economic environment.[12] These changes, as we have discovered, will come as the inevitable result of changes in the economic development of society. The modern growth of capitalism has brought with it the awakening of class-consciousness among the workers, and has also established the majority as the determinant of social good.[13] With this growth has come likewise additional knowledge, new ideas, more accurate social and individual conceptions. Our legislatures and courts, however, have remained consistently hostile to these new conceptions. They fear them as they fear a revolution. In fact they (the conceptions) are revolutionary. "Such a philosophy is impossible, it is pernicious" was the remark of one judge, and he but expressed the common legal sentiment. Voluntarism, or the free-will delusion, after all, when subjected to a final analysis, is a tradition of sound value to any capitalist system.

[11] The only objections we have to Ferri are in connection with his statements as to the fundamental nature and influence of heredity in the production of crime.

[12] And where necessary and possible, of course, in changes in telluric environment, or use of means to change effects of telluric environment.

[13] This, as we show, because it is in accord with the law of social evolution.

The belief that a man, despite adversity of environment, is free to choose his own destiny, and is, therefore, capable of rising to the highest positions in the community, which is the necessary and often repeated implication of the voluntarist creed, is a very satisfactory formula for any status quo.[14] Yet we cannot condemn the judges, as individuals, because they are but inevitably reflecting the ideas of their declining system.

We are now able to approach and answer the questions that were raised at the beginning of the article. The knowledge that all acts are determined, that their expression is as inevitable as the fall of dew or the rush of night, does change our attitude toward moral theories and practices. Acts that are anti-social, as conditions at the time exist, are understood to be as unavoidable as acts that are unquestionably social. The individual who murders a man is no more personally responsible for his deed than a man who erects a library or religious edifice. Both acts are equally inevitable. Responsibility, in the sense that it means that the individual possesses a freedom of choice and might have done differently than he did, is dissolved. To endeavor to evade this fact is futile. Volumes have been written in an attempt to prove that responsibility,

---

[14] The steady decline and burial at least of this phase of voluntarism will come with the demise of capitalism.

as ordinarily conceived, can be retained with acceptance of determinism. Such arguments are largely rationalizations. They are unscientific. An effect cannot be held responsible for its cause, since it is not a product of its making, but is that which is made, itself having no freedom as to its beginning or end. The word responsible is a product of voluntarist ideology. It implies, in dictionary verbiage, a sense of answerability or accountability for one's actions, which in itself is a contradiction since effects cannot be free of their causes.

This conclusion, as inescapable as the logic of numbers, terrifies those students of ethics who fail to see its further extension. Although we cannot hold any man responsible for his actions, that does not mean that we cannot pronounce judgment upon them as to their social value. The actions of one man may be part of a social good, the actions of another part of a social evil. The difference as to what is a social good and what a social evil is determined by the material environment from which the actions arise and are a part. In a system of chattel slavery for a master to kill a slave is a slight, if at all grievous, social evil, but for a slave to kill a master is a grave social offense. The difference in the social character of the offenses is a result of the nature of the social structure. Today the difference is in exact correspondence with the difference between man's social status under slavery and under capitalism. As capitalism concentrates and begins to disintegrate, the majority conception must the more steadily grow into the social consciousness. At present, for instance, though death is the punishment for murder, it is almost a platitude to say that, in proportion to the number of rich and poor who commit the crime, the former but rarely suffer the penalty. It would be illogical, according to the organization of the present system, that it should be otherwise. It would be a contradiction of the law of social evolution. The facility with which the wealthy can be proven insane is a travesty upon *majority justice* that even the ignorant seem to appreciate. Our argument is not against the plea for insanity; the acts of all murderers, if probed as to circumstance and motive, could be shown to be the product of abnormal or subnormal minds; the objection is that the only ones who can succeed in winning such judgment, and by what chicanery often we need not describe, are those who can afford expert attorneys and noted alienists to defend them, and if necessary, pursue their case through the higher courts.[15] Yet, it is necessary to repeat, it would be contradictious

---

[15] A quotation from Darrow's *Crime and Criminals* (pp. 25, 26), is fitting, not because it is phrased in a fashion we approve, or that it possesses the dispassionate character of a scientific document, but because it does have a pertinency and veracity of appeal:
 . . . When your case gets into court it will make little difference "whether you are guilty or innocent; but it's better if you have a smart lawyer. And you cannot have a smart lawyer unless you have

if there were other judgment than this under a system
in which the *majority conception,* however much a fiction, does not have fundamental existence. (Fundamental existence here, means existence that inheres in
the nature of the social system.)

Our judgment as to social values, then, remains, the
repudiation of the idea of responsibility notwithstanding. If a man proves to be a recidivist, and, therefore, according to the ethics of his system, a danger to
society, it is imperative that his conduct be curbed by
some definite and certain action. The necessity of
restraint in no way requires the admission of respon-

money. First and last, it's a question of money. . . . We have no
system for doing justice, not the slightest in the world.

"Let me illustrate: Take the poorest person in this room. If the
community had provided a system of doing justice the poorest person
in this room would have as good a lawyer as the richest, would he
not? When you went into court you would have just as long a trial,
and just as fair a trial as the richest person in Chicago.

"Then, if you were rich and were beaten, your case would be taken
to the Appellate Court. A poor man cannot take his case to the
Appellate Court; he has not the price; and then to the Supreme
Court; and if he were beaten there, he might perhaps go to the
United States Supreme Court. And he might die of old age before
he got into jail. If you are poor, it's a quick job. You are almost
known to be guilty, else you would not be there. Why should any
one be in the Criminal Court if he were not guilty? He would not
be there if he could be anywhere else. The officials have no time to
look after these cases. The people who are on the outside, who are
running banks and building churches and making jails, they have no
time to examine 600 or 700 prisoners each year to see whether they
are guilty or innocent. If the courts were organized to promote
justice, the people would elect somebody to defend all these criminals—somebody as smart as the prosecutor—and give him as many
detectives and as many assistants to help, and pay as much money
to defend you as to prosecute you. We have a very able man for
State's Attorney, and he has many assistants, detectives and police-
men without end, and judges to hear the cases—everything handy."

sibility. The restraint is a purely social expedient. It is the action that the majority must take in order that happiness be insured to the greatest number. An action that is judged as a social evil, that is, an evil for the majority, must be opposed and checked, despite the inevitability of both the judgment and the action. A pyromaniac who on board a crowded steamer sets fire to it undoubtedly is committing an act that in the nature of his nervous system is inevitable, and yet it is of such a devastatingly unsocial character that it is necessary to confine him to places where his incendiarism can do little, if any, harm, and where it may be possible for him to sublimate this impulse. The confinement, which must take on the form of treatment rather than punishment, should be resorted to not because the individual is responsible, or because we in any way blame him for his tendency, but because it is a necessity for social survival. An individual, of frail and sensitive type, while in a rescuing boat tossing on high seas, might be seized with panic, and, in his frenzy, if unrestrained, succeed in capsizing the craft and drowning the passengers. Although his frenzy would be inevitable its effects would be in the nature of a social evil. The action of those who manifested no such frenzied emotion, in contrast, although equally inevitable, would be in the nature of a social good. The judgment as to the badness of the former act and the goodness of the latter is made and determined by the capacity of the act to bring unhappiness or happiness to the greatest number. It is a *majority* judgment.

From the preceding discussion it should be clear that determinism removes the desire for social vengeance. However wicked an act and however necessary it may be to confine its perpetrator in order to prevent its repetition, the fact that it was inevitable, that it was an expression of his personality that was possible of no deviation, creates in us an attitude of understanding and magnanimity. Harshness of judgment and cruelty of restriction become unnecessary as the nature of human reaction is clarified. Recognition of the fact that fear is not the method to cure unsocial actions, that environment is their fundamental cause and the condition that must be altered, changes our tactic. Confinement must only be used, then, as a social measure, for treatment and not for punishment.[16] Jails and prisons must be transformed into hospitals and asylums. The Elmira system, in Elmira, New York, founded and fostered by Dr. Brockway, however super-

---

[16] The word punishment is another word that reflects the voluntarist ideology; it assumes that if an individual is punished for a wrong act he will not do it again, despite the continuance of the causes that drove him to the act. This, as we have shown, is false. Punishment can only be used effectually, and approved, when applied as a means to change or destroy the cause of bad action.

ficial in certain of its deductions as to causes of criminality, is a promising move in that direction.

But hospitals and asylums, reformatories and clinics are but expedient therapeutics. Except as means of treating and discouraging criminality in those who have been detected in criminal activity, they have no preventive effect. They are only necessary because there is disease. It is change of environment only that can act as the efficient preventive.

This change in environment will come with the birth of a new social system, in which the majority, hitherto deprived of authority and treated as a farce or fiction, will be the determinant of social good. In previous stages of society, where, in order that the species might progress, it was impossible for the majority to act as this determinant, it was but natural to expect the narrow and barbarous practices that history has recorded. It is only the sentimentalist or utopian who is shocked at these historical inhumanities. The understanding and appreciation of determinism in all of its far-reaching economic and psychological aspects could only have come with the development of capitalism, which brought with it a great and newer kind of *production*,[17]

[17] Spinoza's determinism, perfect in its origin, found escape in his theory of intuitional knowledge, which was tantamount to a form of mystical ecstasy, and even D'Holbach, living in the days when feudalism was on the verge of wreck, did not see the expression of determinism in the economic history of society. Kant likewise, although he declared the freedom of being determined by one's own

the doctrine of surplus value could not have been conceived under any other system; the idea of the inevitable, with its scientific implications, could not have come into acceptance or been proved without the growth of modern science, which was possible of important advance only with the rise of the capitalist industrial system. The rise and decline of a system is a matter of material necessity. A system may be bad in an immediate sense, but good in an historical sense, and vice versa. Socialism should not be argued from a moral but a necessitarian point of view; the former is utopian, the latter scientific. Individual action must be considered as inevitable as changes in society or variations in respiration, and their value or disvalue, goodness or badness, be examined in reference to their effects upon the majority of the populace. This is a judgment, of course, that assumes the existence of a socialist state where the majority has actually advanced to its real position as determinant of the social good; and any

ideas is in truth no better than the freedom of a roasting-jack, which, being once set going, produces its movements by itself, failed to see that his transcendentalism was a patent refutation of precisely this statement. Taine, also, with all of the logic and brilliance of *De l'Intelligence,* only caught glimpses of the extensive implications of the truth for which he so eloquently argued. Nor did the positivist Claude Bernard, the author of that famous sentence, *"Il y a un determinisme absolu, dans les conditions d'existence des phenomenes naturels, aussi bien pour les corps vivants que pour les corps bruts,"* recognize that the determinism that he wrote about involved certain specific social characteristics which no complete determinist philosophy can neglect.

socialist system in which the majority cannot so act is certain to fail. It is this correlation between the ascent of the majority and the development and change of productive forces and their management that is the important stage in social evolution which cannot be disregarded. Only this correlative ascent and change will make majority judgment a reality and not a fiction. Only this correlation will make morals or ethics an accurate reflection of the majority purpose.

THE GREAT MAN ILLUSION

THE problem of the great man has usually been hidden in a mist of conjecture and superstition. It has seldom been attacked with success. The approach has too often been worshipful instead of analytic. Complexity of situation has caused confusion of attitude. Scientists—and philosophers—have usually handled the problem with tender-tipped fingers. It is our purpose in this essay not to provide a final solution of the problem, but to indicate the correct manner of approach if such a solution is ever to be attained.[1] In the beginning we shall deal with the broad and general features of the problem and thence proceed to the minute and particular.

Geniuses or great men, despite William James, who declared that we "must simply accept geniuses as data," spontaneous inexplicable outgrowths that is, are just as much the product of causes, definite enough if once observed, as an idea is or a whirlwind. Greatness implies a going beyond—a standing out—an achieving of that which seems impossible to be achieved by other

---

[1] Since the appearance of this article (February, 1923) the author has been informed by Professor Richter of the Johns Hopkins University Medical School that experiments of the kind suggested in the latter part of this essay are being tried in his laboratory-clinic.

minds. It is more—it is an achieving in those endeavors that men approve and value and which have the most use to the human race (Singing, for example, though it has no practical use in increasing the bread supply of a nation still has use in that it pleases the senses and hence heightens the value of existence—singing can only become "most useful" when most people can hear it and most people are able to appreciate its beauty.) The idea of looking upon greatness as a mystery or an accident is as absurd as the attitude of the medieval scholastics who opposed the dissection of the body on the ground that the resurrection-bone would be destroyed. The circumstances which in their peculiar manifestations provided the opportunity and made it possible for certain men to become great, though composite, are not too mystifying for observation and study. It is not difficult in the life of every great man to indicate certain conditions and circumstances, frequently a condition or circumstance upon which the expression of his greatness depended. In the case of Shakespeare, as Helvetius has remarked, had not a series of circumstances, all connected, occurred, his greatness, as one speaks of it, would unquestionably have remained unknown. If he had remained a woolen merchant like his father or had his bad conduct not forced him to leave the business, or had he not associated with libertines and later been pursued for his theft of a horse, and been obliged to fly to London and enter the stage he would never have become the leading and distinguished English dramatist. His ability, latent to a degree, as that of all men is, was mainly developed, at any rate stimulated to utterance, by the conditions that favored him.

There is nothing mysterious or inscrutable about these conditions. They are facts that can be studied as objects the same as mobs or stones. To study a thing as an object implies a complete knowledge of that thing; for instance we study rivers as objects— even though their waters change at frequent intervals, run at different rates according to depth and level, carry different materials at different points, and bifurcate and finally ramify into labyrinths of streams and rivulets—because we know their origin, their relation with surrounding things, their several curious characteristics of growth and decline and can determine them with reasonable accuracy. Man's sensory mechanism and nervous organization are intricate, variant in behaviour, baffling now as to particular forms of expression, but by no means beyond handling as objects. To get these reactions reduced to a quantitative basis is the end to be worked toward. Every river varies, as does every tree, mountain, or rock, but it can be studied scientifically, classified and understood so fully in both origin and growth that with little difficulty we can predict what will be its change and form next month or next century. The geologic circumstances that go to make a river are multiple but essentially not more complex than those, in human affairs, that go to shape an individual. Excessive rainfall, and vapor and fogs when condensed, form rills, and if continued, by erosion, produce furrows; these rills by uniting form rivulets which excavate gullies and these rivulets uniting with one another and with streamlets, form torrents which eat away ravines and gorges and finally these torrents converging and uniting form great rivers which succeed in beating their way to the sea. Now to men! Certain men are born into impoverished households, nurtured on cheap and unwholesome food, reared in careless, thoughtless and unnatural ways, educated improperly and insufficiently, then forced into factories to work as drudges; all these circumstances working feverishly toward a point of rebellion, hastened often by early and overly fecund marriages or undue stress brought about by illness or unemployment, produce criminals of types varying according to the intensity of their antecedent conditions. Other men born into fairly comfortable houses, nurtured on not unhealthful food, reared in less careless and thoughtless manners, educated less improperly and a deal more fully, then forced into less distasteful and arduous work, unencumbered by overly large families or seriously affected by the fluctuations of labor, produce flabby, bourgeois citizens of degrees varying slightly according to the slight differences in their early environment. Other men, born on sumptuous estates, nurtured on carefully prepared food, reared cautiously and thoughtfully, educated a good deal less improperly and a very great deal more fully, then allowed to choose their own vocations or at least permitted certain flexibility of choice, and happily furnished with a series of advantages, produce busy financiers, famous statesmen, and well-known scientists. Between all three of these types there are numerous exceptions, none, however, from other than perfectly patent and comprehensible causes. Ample statistics, those of Odin especially, have proven that over ninety-five per cent of the famous men of the world have had a wide and reasonably inclusive education, gotten either in a university or through assiduity of private study, which clearly demonstrates that of the millions that go uneducated every generation there is but the very slightest chance that they may achieve any high degree of distinction. The causes that make the men, or at all events a certain percentage of the men, of the first group criminals or sadly warped proletarians, the second group thickly set bourgeois citizens, and the third rich masters of industry and government, are definite enough at first sight, and intricate study could show precisely what variations of their particular environment made them different.

With the exceptions difficulty mounts. Robert Burns, a peasant, was known as a village celebrity at sixteen and as a famous poet at twenty-seven. His peasant genius is startling, and at first glimpse seems to defy analysis. Yet we know that his father was careful to give him as well as his brothers and sisters a good education, or at any rate a much better one than that received by most farmers' sons in Scotland. At five years he had been sent to school at Alloway Mill, and when the family moved the father employed a young and thoughtful instructor by the name of Murdoch who gave the children a quite interesting and thorough elementary education, which included a precise study of words and verse, particularly the forms of the latter. Later, when Murdoch migrated, the father himself undertook with unusual paternal conscientiousness to continue this education into higher subjects. A not inconsiderable collection of books, including the works of Shakespeare, Pope, Locke, Boyle, and Allan Ramsay, was always at Burns' command. At fifteen a certain circumstance promoted his ambition and awoke in him the desire to be a poet. The girl who inspired *Handsome Nell,* his initial poem, was the first to give him the necessary encouragement to actually compose. She sang a song which she said had been written by a country laird's son whom Burns knew; hitherto Burns had believed that only men learned in Greek and Latin were really able to write poetry, but, seeing that a country laird's son could rhyme fairly well, he concluded that there was no reason why he could not do the same. This episode Burns relates in one of his letters. In 1785, the same as in 1784, the crops failed, and these failures, especially the last, forced him to idleness and introspection. This circumstance, seemingly unfortunate, actually gave him leisure time to develop his poetic talent. Later another circumstance brought to print his first volume of poems. Pursued by the police, whom Jean Armour's father had set after him, Burns planned to go to Jamaica as a bookkeeper in the employ of Mr. Douglas, and, lacking money for passage, Gavin Hamilton suggested that he publish his poems as a means of getting it. The book succeeded. However, because of the various changing dates of sailing which discouraged him and because of his constantly growing fame, Burns suddenly decided not to exile himself from Scotland. Obviously, had it not been due to the necessity of the moment, brought about by Jean's father, Burns might never have wanted to go to Jamaica and his poems might never have been printed. At any rate, another necessity, or even a desire, that might have urged their publication undoubtedly would have come at a later time, and that Burns would have responded in a different, perhaps less enthusiastic and productive, way is without question. To search even deeper, had not Burns inherited a certain excess of sex passion and had not certain conditions and circumstances in his life irritated this into such frequent and changing expression, the best of his love poems would never have been written. More than one Burns, with passions inherently as high-tempered and with capacity not less brilliant, have met with other conditions and by them been pressed into other vocations discouraging to the growth of their talent.

Any circumstance in Burns' life could be taken and the effect it had upon his poetry be shown. An accumulation of varying circumstances reacting on a readily plastic nature create certain tendencies which crave a form of expression; this found, and continued, a resultant complex, to speak in the language of modern thought, or habit-pattern, is built up that in time insists upon and demands just this particular way of manifesting itself. This is true as well of the man who in distress takes to smoking and later, through continuance of the habit, will not be without a cigar, as it is of the man who in love or pain takes to writing, and through certain repeated circumstances later will not get relief or satisfaction except by taking up his pen. Essentially the habits are different only in form and intensity; in terms of the nervous system and brain response they have a fundamental likeness.

All genius, as well as everything else in man, originally had to come from external stimuli—conditions. Pythagoras surpassed the other Greeks of Iona and later at Crotona simply because certain conditions in his life (and by life we include his heredity), reacting on his exceedingly impressionable nature, which also was the product of certain early conditions, made it possible for his mind to grow and see beyond the others who had existed or suffered under conditions less propitious. Likewise Robert Burns became a remarkable poet because the conditions in his life molded him into something finer and more responsive than the other people about him. *These conditions can be discovered.* Partially they are already known. The futility of past and present thought has largely been due to its concentrated study of effects, which are but manifestations, without searching with any great seriousness into their etiology. That the scientists too often leave for the divines, the mystics, and peripatetics. Had not Burns' father been interested in educating his children and employed Murdoch, for instance, who taught them the forms and tricks of verse, Robert Burns in all likelihood would never have been a poet. He might have sung ballads, even made them up as he sang, but never would have achieved greatness with his rhymes. He would never have known what great poetry really was nor the ways of writing it.

This brings us to another illusion: Burns would have educated himself if his father had not provided a teacher for him and later instructed him himself. No man has ever had a desire for anything except as outside stimuli have excited and aroused it. Were man's social heritage suddenly taken from him he would no more desire to read than today he wants to count pebbles on a beach. The desire to read is a thing quite removed from his natural impulse (the desire to know likewise is a product of conditions dependent upon obstacles, and becomes insistent according to the insistency of the conditions; the Brazilian is not half so anxious "to know" as the German); the desire to eat and protect himself from the attacks of climate, disease and death, and to seek sexual expression, on the other hand, he would have, the same as in a less complex way the earthworm has or the frog. The desire to read is a desire invented by man in his struggle to combat conditions, the same as speech is or machinery. It is perpetuated by systematically constructed environment—accordingly as it is encouraged it grows. Encouragement involves many factors. Certain characteristics of ancestry must be considered. One savage, accustomed to interpreting a more developed stage of picture writing which had been transmitted to him by his tribe, will be able to seize upon the meaning of a beginning phonetic form more quickly than another savage whose tribe has not advanced beyond the first representations of picture writing. Likewise a youth, whose family has risen to a position of acquaintance with intellectual things, will be able to appreciate the meaning of education more rapidly than a youth whose family has never known more than the bare rudiments of knowledge. The encouragement in the instance of the first savage and the first youth lies not in themselves but in the progress that their respective tribe and family have made, which ultimately reduces itself to a discussion of the causal-conditions that made it possible for their tribe and family to be in advance of those of the latter savage and youth. In other words, it is the same as the reason or reasons why Buckle could write the *History of Civilization in England* in three volumes and other men, potentially as profound as Buckle but born into less encouraging environments, could not write either it or anything else. Buckle was born into a family that encouraged his education; further, he had the means of getting an education, he had an income that saved him from an arduous struggle for existence, and he had the leisure time requisite for such work.

Burns, then, or anyone, would not, could not, have educated himself had it not been for the original stimuli that stirred the desire. To repeat, no child placed alone in a forest would seek an education. The stimuli have to come from outside the person. In the case of Burns, the underlying stimuli were the desire of his father to have his children educated and the inspiration of Murdoch—the subtler stimuli are instanced in the affair with *Handsome Nell;* those which developed the hyperactive nature of his sexual instinct, and made him so sensitive to slight impressions, though the sublest are those which only scientific study of Burns' life can discover. Burns could not have sung words had not his people taught them to him. No man can think clearly and profoundly if he is not taught language and writing. No man can become great, therefore, unless the necessary stimuli are afforded him.

At present, investigation has not gone far enough to tell with precision the subtler combinations of stimuli that promote genius and not until human reactions are reduced to a more quantitative basis will it be possible to discover them, as today we have discovered the alpha and beta particles, the helium and hydrogen nuclei, that constitute matter, a thing that was considered "beyond the range of human intelligence" two decades ago. But the certain outstanding conditions, which are stimuli in a broad sense, that make genius possible and which work toward the increase of it, are indisputably known at present.

First, economic conditions. Men, it is true, have risen from impoverished homes to positions of distinction and have become, like Faraday and Pasteur, intellectual giants. But these have been the exceptions. And these, Faraday, Pasteur, Bunyan, etc., all met with stimuli that were favorable to their development and which others of their class of the same capacity did not meet—Bunyan, for instance, mentions in his autobiography that "despite the meanness and inconsiderableness of my parents it pleased God to put it into their hearts to put me to school to learn me both to read and to write." And Bunyan's experience in the world led him inevitably to religion where his wild emotionalism, the product of these early riotous experiences, found full flow. Without having been put to school and without having had the experiences he had, *Pilgrim's Progress* would never have been produced. But the struggle was terribly difficult, and had certain stimuli veered even slightly, as in the case of Burns they might so easily have done, the result would have been failure. Even Faraday and Pasteur did their best scientific study only when their economic conditions had reached the stage where they had a laboratory equipped with more than improvised instruments. The multitude of others with whom the stimuli did veer, or showed no favors at all, could not even struggle. If Darwin had not taken his trip on the *Beagle,* which only by a chance did occur, *The Origin of Species* and *Descent of Man* might never have been written, or at all events would have been written differently, no doubt less effectively. But had Darwin not had the economic means to carry on his biological research afterwards, with even more certainty it can be said that *The Origin of Species* and *Descent of Man* would never have been written—any more than Herbert Spencer could have carried on his studies to such a point of success, or have written so voluminously and well had not it been for a legacy left him by his uncle in 1853, without which he himself in his autobiography admitted he "should not have been able to write the *Principles of Psychology*." Economic conditions then do more to make great men possible than the divine afflatus. When favorable economic conditions become more widespread, by the very law of averages, if by no other criterion, the number of great men must increase.

Secondly, education. Education is dependent upon economic conditions. An uneducated man living under the best of economic conditions cannot become great—though the best of economic conditions would stimulate a desire for education. (Education of course does not necessarily mean that derived from schools and colleges, for it can just as well be knowledge acquired through private study and observation.) D'Alembert could not have become a famous mathematical genius had he not been sent to school and trained in the elements of mathematics, any more than Columbus could have discovered America had he never gone to sea. Education is a prerequisite to intellectual greatness the same as the knowledge of drill and military tactics is a prerequisite to gaining martial distinction. And the forms of greatness today that are not to a considerable extent intellectual are none. Then to make it possible for all people to become educated is the immediate problem. Education has been the cry of almost all leaders from sociologists to statesmen. The state even makes a certain degree of education compulsory. But all this is avoiding the crux of the problem. As was signified in one of the preceding paragraphs, a desire for education is a thing created by environment. It arises from certain stimuli in the environment. School is only one form of such stimuli. The school stimulus can be effective only when not forced to combat stimuli too strongly opposite in tendency. The first youth, described above, who was born into a family acquainted with intellectual things, was afforded stimuli encouraging to the school stimulus, and had created in him a desire for education, which really became a habit response, as the second youth, subjected to exactly the same school stimulus yet reared among people and surroundings that afforded nothing but discouragement to this school stimulus, did not have created in him. In other words, more than the mere school stimulus is needed to awaken a desire for education in an individual—with some the school stimulus alone apparently was strong enough to overcome untoward stimuli, but these some were exceptions. And these were exceptions only because either the untoward stimuli were not untoward enough, or the school stimulus, in the form of an extraordinarily inspiring teacher, had an effect more subtle and stimulating than usual. To speak more concretely, a child living in a home where he is made to know that he is being sent to school only until he is confirmed or reaches the age limit that grants him a work permit, has about one chance in thousands of being sufficiently affected by the school stimulus to have a real desire for knowledge aroused in him. You have to change his home environment which, acting as one of the most potent stimuli in his life, limits him in his endeavors. Therefore, the "education-as-a-panacea" cry can mean little to the great mass of children until the inhibiting stimuli, now the inevitable concomitants of their environment, are removed. A change in educational opportunity, therefore, can result only from a change in economic environment.

None the less, good economic conditions and good educational facilities do not alone produce great men— they make easy the way for the appearance of great men. They are necessary if society is to progress in any great sense. But peculiar inherited mental combinations, which are as much the result of previous stimuli as mitotic changes in a nucleus, and more peculiar environmental influences are the immediate causes. Choose a definite example! A man is a gifted musician. His playing reveals profound emotion and miraculous command of technique. "A born genius, a divine product," is the common exclamation, which is not far removed from the ideas of James and Carlyle. Yet his genius can be reduced to several fundamental factors. His ear is marvelously keen; it can detect infinitesimal modulations of tone; his instinct for rhythm is pronounced to a high degree; his sense of melody is as perfect as a trained marksman's eye; his fingers are deft and nimble and have a tactile sensitiveness that is distinctly abnormal. All these combined create his musical genius. Or we might turn to painting. A painter must have an eye as keen for color as a musician's ear for tone; he must possess a knowledge of line and form and a sense of perspective; he must be sensitive to impressions that might escape another man, and be able to record them on canvas; his touch must be delicate, and there might be enumerated a group of other, less important, characteristics, that he ought to possess. Now all these qualities, which are the prerequisites of the great musician or great painter, the same as the desire for knowledge, or to go to more common things, the philatelic's desire for stamps or the numismatic's desire for coins, are results of certain external stimuli. They have to be! A stamp collector could never have existed had not stamps been printed, nor a coin collector been possible had not coins been made; any more than a musician could exist were there not such things as tone, rhythm, and melody, or a painter if there were not color and form. If an individual lives where he frequently hears music or sees painting, especially in the process of creation, he is undoubtedly more likely to become musical or artistic than an individual who hears or sees neither, or at least comes in contact with them very infrequently. Some men have keen ears for tone though they are not musicians, and some have not. This keenness could not have come by itself, inspirationally; it had to come from some stimulus or stimuli. The same is true with melody—of rhythm there will be a full account later. A man can only develop a high sense of discrimination for tone, rhythm, and melody, if he comes into contact with the proper tonal, rhythmic, and melodic stimuli. But such qualities are more frequently inherited than acquired will be an immediate rejoinder. Yet did not the person or persons from whom these individuals inherited these qualities have to meet with these stimuli somewhere in their experience in order to transmit them —or stimuli, though unconscious to the individuals, that would approximate them? Can a grinding machine sew stitches? Can a man multiply without a knowledge of numbers?—or contract tuberculosis without being infected with tubercular germs? Certain aural stimuli repeated made one man's ear more sensitive to tones than another's whose ear did not experience these stimuli or at all events not so repeatedly or strongly. The same is true with rhythm and melody as it is also with color and form. If we could postulate a state where individuals could exist without stimuli, there you would find everyone's eye for color, except in cases of congenital deficiency of vision, absolutely equal—as soon as stimuli began to act, difference of sensitiveness to them, according to the difference of the stimuli, would result. The ultraviolet light now cannot be seen by the human eye, because the wave lengths are shorter than those that affect the eye ordinarily, but it is quite conclusive that if you let a man live for a number of years in a room filled with nothing but ultraviolet light, he would, in time, be able to perceive it the same as he now sees blue or after he is in an unlighted room for considerable time he can make out objects which when he first entered were obscured from his sight. The matter of tone would be much simpler. That stimuli alone, transmitted or acquired, make all these differences will not be denied—unless we blame it on a convenient other-world monarch.

Now what can be done with this knowledge? Granted that great men are different from ordinary men only in that they have experienced different stimuli, indirectly or directly, or both, is this knowledge at all useful? We know that a gifted musician has a keen ear, a highly developed sense of rhythm and melody, a deft touch, etc., and know that these are, that they have to be, the results of certain stimuli. Still how can we know these stimuli, and the combinations with which they work, to such a point of exactitude that they will be of practical value to us? There are two ways of doing this: first, by experiment, and, second, by scientific biography.

Since certain aural stimuli had to develop the keenness of hearing characteristic of the musician, our first experimenting could well begin with the ear, assuming, of course, for the sake of following the above comparisons, that we should want to locate the particular stimuli necessary to create musical genius. In any experiments of this type we should have to deal with children of the very youngest age possible, that is, at a time when the fewest stimuli have had an opportunity to affect them. Even among these children, those as young as six months as well as those of thirty-six months, there will be perceptible differences of response, the differences being proportionally greater according to the advancing age. By experience with sound every one of these children can be taught to distinguish nuances of tone that at present escape the average individual, the same as a painter can detect a variation in composition so small that other observers cannot perceive the least hint of it. Some children may be able to perceive these tonal differences more quickly and to more minute points than others, because of their inherited susceptibility to sound—one of their fathers may have been a pianist, another a piano-tuner, or of other occupation that evoked aural keenness. The Indian scouts of older days developed an ability to detect the faintest echo in a forest, while the men back in camp might not have been able to hear a rustle of leaves ten yards away. It was experience with sound and the adaptability of the ear to the stimulus that made the difference. Yet certain scouts were keener than others—certainly if one's father were a scout, and had his own ears constantly trained from childhood up, he would be more likely to detect infinitesimal sounds than one who became a scout only by chance at the age of twenty or thirty. Likewise with children and music, as has been shown. Particular forms of motivation also are expedient—the scout's hearing is heightened somewhat by the knowledge that there are at least hundreds of lives dependent upon his alertness; the child by being taught to realize the importance of tonal values will become more interested and apt. Stimuli

[235]

can be so adjusted and the conditions in which they
are given made so conducive to whatever the experi-
menter may desire, that it is not rash to say that where
today one child in a thousand has "an ear for tone"
tomorrow hundreds in a thousand may be made to have
such.

Exactly the same type of work can be done with the
problem of rhythm. Rhythm is really the fundament
of music. It is from rhythm that the musical impulse
originally sprang. Its temporal primacy is not to be
contested. It is because rhythm is so directly connected with the functioning of the nervous system that
it is so instinctive. The human organism is built upon
a rhythmic basis: the pulse-beats, the systole and
diastole of the heart, the regularity of inspiration and
expiration, the activity of certain of the glands, aside
from such obvious phenomena as walking and talking,
are convincing proof of the fact. The susceptibility of
an individual then to external rhythmic stimuli is determined by two factors: first, the nature of his constitutional rhythmic reactions (rhythmic rate of circula-
tion of blood, etc.), and secondly, by the stimuli he has
met with which have encouraged or discouraged this
tendency. In the case of the first of these factors
progress can be made by the study of the physiological
character of children with the purpose of discovering
their native rhythmic responses, and, by locating the

physical causes that make them abnormally or sub-normally active, see to what extent they can be changed for the benefit of the individual—provided such change for the purpose desired is imperative. At any rate those children most sensitive to rhythmic stimuli could be selected, and work in cultivation of this very pronounced tendency which they possess be made as scientific as a chemical experiment. In the matter of the second of these factors the task is more simple. Those stimuli that encourage or discourage rhythmic response can be ascertained as accurately as those which encourage or discourage eating, sleeping, or any number of other purely physical acts. By study of these stimuli and by practice of them on children it will be possible to develop greater and greater sensitiveness to rhythm dependent upon the constitutional character of the child and the fittingness of the stimuli employed. Repetition of the stimuli will be necessary. It may be that specific work with the metronome or with a tom-tom can produce rhythmic responses more valuable than those transmitted through three generations of inheritance.

With melody the same can be done, and also with the matter of form and color. All these are problems of stimuli. How did certain cave-men come to draw rhinoceroses with such marvelous perfection of line, while other cave-men, not forced to the life of the former and unaccustomed to their utensils, could barely sketch an eye? Did a spiritual being guide their hands? Hardly! The cause then must have been those stimuli that first gave direction to such a reaction. It may have been a glacial invasion that forced certain of them to a prolonged life in their caves, or a chance discovery of chalk, charcoal, or other drawing objects, or a belief that if they could make a rhinoceros on the wall of the cave that animal might save them, or in another case, might keep from molesting them—any of a multitude of possible causes might have first acted as the stimulus. Its frequency would develop more efficient responses, etc. So it is with all the qualities that make great men—the stimuli that made them can be discovered through experiment and analysis and this knowledge can be applied in order to bring about an increase of these qualities.

The author who writes a story of a play possesses qualities just as definite and subject to analysis as those of a musician or an artist. As was said above, by experiment it is possible to discover what particular stimuli make it so easy for certain children to draw beautifully straight or curved lines or have such an intuition for color blends, the same as it is possible to find what stimuli make them draw crooked lines, etc., and thus by wider application of these first stimuli, and those stimuli concomitant with art-creation, we should be able to produce more and greater artists.

[238]

The same is true with any art and with any science. With style in literature this can be done the same as with form in art. And content or substance likewise is no more unsubject to such analysis. This will mean a development of psychology far beyond its present stage—psychology by study of man as an object (of course psychology here involves many sciences that are really part of it) will be able to measure reaction-time and stimulus-effect in the way in which at present we measure the speed of an invisible proton.

When it is said, therefore, that Shakespeare is the greatest writer in the world because his knowledge of human nature was so various and profound, or because he was the master of such sublime thought, what we in causal terms have said is that Shakespeare came into contact with those stimuli, those experiences if you will, that, reacting on his nature, could but inevitably make him the man and author he was. And that these stimuli, with the advance of science which will enable man to study himself as an object, and which can be brought about most rapidly by a study of early environment, a thing possible only under conditions that afford ample time for such study, can be known even to their subtlest manifestations. As was pointed out previously, there was a time when matter was viewed as impossible of analysis—the days before Thomson—the same as the human body was considered too divine a mechanism to ever reveal its secrets to man. Science since then, it is almost bromidic to say, his disproved the putative validity of such assumptions. Certain stimuli such as favorable economic conditions and education, as has been shown above, are conducive to greatness, they make it easier to develop; other stimuli are likewise conducive though not so well nor so fully known. Experiment and scientific biography have been indicated as the methods of discovering these. Of the nature of these experiments there has been discussion in the above paragraphs. Of the nature of Scientific Biography we shall speak in the succeeding paragraph.

Scientific Biography can become one of the most important and illuminating studies that exist. Biography and criticism hitherto have been impressionistic largely; they have tried to entertain and at the same time be accurate, but they have rarely tried to search for causes or interpret their relations. Biography has been so futile in its dealing with great men, statesmen as well as artists and scientists, because it has taken and looked upon them as above and beyond the influence of conditions, as the makers of conditions, in fact, rather than the products of them. This is a false premise; all scientific evidence proves it to be false. Men become great through causes that are directly through environment or indirectly through heredity the product of conditions. Evolution could take place only through the directing stimuli of environment. Heredity itself is a product of conditions; and certainly if conditions can be altered heredity can be altered. Once it would have taken hundreds of years to build the Panama Canal; in our own day it was done in almost half a decade; once it took man centuries to make himself immune to certain disease germs; today he makes antitoxins (diphtheric, typhoid, smallpox) that revolutionize the process—he no longer has to wait centuries. It is not inconceivable that man, when his knowledge of chromosomic transmission is more complete, will eventually devise means to hasten or hinder the process of heredity. At any rate his labors are in that direction.

When biographers realize these things the first positive step in the direction of scientific biography will have been taken. Not before! Then biography will become a matter of studying the causal stimuli or, largely speaking, conditions that make or have made it possible for men to become great, and not the depiction of how, despite all difficulties and obstacles, great men conquer circumstances and ride triumphantly to success.

"Thomas . . . was always a studious and progressive youth; while other boys were dawdling away their time at games and reading worthless books he was selling newspapers on trains in order to make enough money to continue his education. This same progressiveness, this remarkable exuberance of energy characterized him throughout his life and made so deserved the success that crowned his efforts. Other youths, continuing their indolent habits, seldom achieved a success in the least comparable to his. Which all goes to prove how necessary it is that we teach our youths to be diligent and hard-working and avoid the soft tempting ways of idleness that always lead to failure, distress, and often to disgrace."

This is no exaggeration of the type of didactic biography—it is mawkish and sentimental because its method and theory are mawkish and sentimental. It is superficial, wabbly, unsubstantial biography—it is satisfied with recording and little more. Its attempts at interpretation are feeble and futile. Scientific biography, on the other hand, would be more than interpretive—it would be causal, which necessarily means profound. It would not preach, but analyze the preaching process. It would not say because a man is diligent and energetic he therefore will or ought to succeed far beyond his less diligent and energetic associates; but it will search into the lives of this man and those men to discover the causes or stimuli, if we choose, that made this man so diligent and energetic and those men the opposite. It will not say that George Washington was greater than Benedict Arnold, because, in the face of all distress and discouragement, he remained faithful to the American army and led it to victory, while Arnold with but slight provocation deserted; but it will probe into the conditions that affected these men individually, perceive their relations direct or indirect to past conditions and thus discover the specific nature of the causes that made the one stalwart and unwavering, and the other hyper-sensitive and easily swerved. It would, then, show quite conclusively, not how Washington rose above conditions to success, but how conditions, coming in certain favorable combinations, rode him to success. From these evidences, culled from a multitude of biographies, which would require persevering, tireless, but fruitful work, actual laws of individual progress will be derived. Indeed that fuzzy-minded English critic, whom we have noted several times beside William James and who so blindly interpreted history as the achievements of great men, still had passing insight enough to get a glimpse of scientific biography when he wrote: "Of a truth, it is the duty of all men, especially of all philosophers, to note down with accuracy the characteristic circumstances of their education, what furthered, what hindered, what in any way modified it." The words quoted are of much greater significance than they at first appear.

To recapitulate—already we have discovered the importance of such factors as economic conditions and education, and what they can do to promote genius; still the matter of the less obvious and less tangible stimuli concerned in the problem have to be solved. Experiment with children before the mass stimuli of life have begun to shape their lives is the most direct and thorough method. These experiments will be more important than any that have been attempted in the past. They will reveal the incalculable importance of early environment—why, for instance, J. S. Mill could know Greek at three, Jeremy Bentham Latin at four, or Mozart the clavier at five, while others know none of them at twelve. They will supply convincing evidence why education should begin at birth almost, or at any rate not long after a child has finished suckling, instead of at six when the most formative period of its life has passed. Prodigies of the Mill, Bentham, Mozart types will become more explicable and reproducible phenomena. As experiments progress it will be possible to establish laws for stimuli more precise and definite than the law of association or Weber's law. Not many years ago dreams were looked upon as being as unaccountable as typhoons were once considered. They were even thought to be phantasmal, prophetic, devoid of antecedent causes. Just as one time philosophers denied the idea of regularity in the material world, so even psychologists, until this generation, denied the law of cause and effect in dreams. It is always easier to fall back on Tyche than cause. It is always easier to blame things on generalities than reduce them to their origins. It is more convenient to speak of brotherliness and peace than it is to go to the economic causes that will make them actual and enduring. It is less difficult to blame things on the immutable past than to delve into the causes that made that past seemingly so immutable and the future so fully dependent on it. When J. S. Mill wrote "of all vulgar modes of escaping from the consideration of the effect of social and moral influences on the human mind, the most vulgar is that of attributing the diversities of conduct and character to inherent natural differences" he was openly assailing one of the most harmful forms of that tendency. Present social conditions encourage this invasion and superficiality. Science itself cannot see far enough beyond the immediacy of experiment to coördinate its discoveries, or see in what way they point, and labor in that direction. Experiments then, as important as those urged above, cannot become, in any complete sense, effectual until this attitude is changed. Cause and effect cannot be divorced. The scientist cannot do great work unless he has a consciousness of the scope and significance of his task—

neither can the philosopher, the theologian, the literary critic, who assert their independence of experiment and reason.

Scientific Biography should discourage this narrowness. Experiment should remove it.

THE RISE OF OBJECTIVE PSYCHOLOGY

COMTE was not the first to maintain that psychology could never develop into a science. Nor was he the last! It is curious to note the numerous shiftings of opinion made by so many philosophers in this argument. In the entire problem, however, there has been rarely, if ever, a clear defining of the issues, and in no case an attempt made to describe exactly what is supposed to be science and what not. A floundering in hazy and meaningless terminology has resulted, with no definite advance in objective knowledge.

Lange put the difficulty quite succinctly in his *History of Materialism,* and a quotation from his statement on the subject is distinctly pertinent:

"In psychology we can undertake no dissections, can weigh and measure nothing, can exhibit no preparations. Names like thinking, feeling, willing, are mere names. Who will point out exactly what corresponds to them? Shall we make definitions? A treacherous element! They are of no use, at least for any exact comparisons. And with what are we to connect our observations? With what measure shall we measure? In this groping in the dark it is only childish prejudice or the clairvoyant impulse of the metaphysician that is sure of finding anything. The understanding has only one way: it can only compare the positive, attested, observed actions of the animal world with their organs. It must resolve the question into the question of modes and causes of motion."

The problem, though not realized by most, immediately resolves itself into a discussion of the nature of objective and subjective knowledge and their relations to science. Objective knowledge, loosely described, is that knowledge which is acceptable by all, that is universal, and true for all times. Subjective knowledge, loosely described, is personal knowledge, knowledge that is not acceptable by all and hence not universal, and does not have to be true for all times.

Knowledge must be defined as ideas of objects; the objects, it is assumed, are those things, in fact all things, that exist outside of us and can affect us, and ideas the mental replicas of these objects in the brain in such a way that awareness of their existence results. Essentially, then, all knowledge is subjective, since whatever is known must be known first through individuals, that is, personally, before it can attain an objective status. The most objective piece of knowledge in the universe is none the less personal or subjective in its acceptance by every individual. Whatever is known, of course, working from a purely Lockian basis, must be known by sensitive things; we cannot conceive of insensate things, matter itself in other words, having knowledge, and therefore it follows that were it not for sensitive things there would be no knowledge, as we define knowledge, in the world.

To the degree that men can acquiesce as to the nature of an object does the knowledge of it become "objective." What is strictly meant is that we get close enough to the object to derive sufficient knowledge of it for all men, able to get the same knowledge, to agree as to its nature. With what is usually called subjective knowledge, this is not true. Now what is it that distinguishes objective knowledge from subjective? *The object is there in either case;* it must be there in all cases, or there could be no knowledge. But in the one case we are able to come to definite agreement as to the major qualities of the object—it must be observed here that that does not include the "why and wherefore" or the *ding an sich*—while in the other there is wide, personal disagreement, or what is commonly known as subjective opinion.

The difference between objective and subjective knowledge is due to the fact that in the former there exists an accepted system of coördinates or means of measurement, while in the latter no such means are at hand—and there are important reasons why they are not at hand. This point requires further illustration. A picture exists just as definitely and precisely as the

moon; a piece of mica is fundamentally no more definite an object than a phrase or symphony concert;
they are all objects capable of affecting us. It is true
that the effects of a picture or a symphony concert
upon the nervous system are more complex than the
effects of the moon or the mica, but that does not
mean that they are not just as much open to study as
the former.

Let us raise the question again as to why the knowledge of the moon, the mica, or the gravitational tendency of the universe, for further example, is viewed as
objective, and the knowledge of the picture, the symphony concert, and, to add another instance, the religious impulse, is viewed as subjective. The solution
is simple. In the first case we have knowledge that
can be got in a uniform manner by all with no chance
of disagreement, while in the second case the knowledge
is not got in a uniform manner and as a consequence
is conceived differently and is held to be subjective.
The knowledge in the case of the moon, the mica,
gravity, etc., is got the same by all because they have
definite measurements with which to work. In other
words, they can measure the breadth, length, and thickness of the object because they have metric or linear
scales as an accepted basis. They can tell the compressibility or expansibility of an object because they
have definite coördinates from which to compute. They

can tell "objectively," if you will, the nature of visual reaction with opthalmoscopes and the character of kidney function with cystoscopes. They can tell exactly how far an amœba will move by means of micrometers or what paths an electron follows by an electroscope. Only by these methods could science have progressed to the place that it has. All knowledge comes through comparison and without these means of measurement comparison could never be made exact, and that means acceptable by all. Were it not for the micrometer, for instance, knowledge of how far a certain amœba moved under a certain stimulus, or what size it assumed when it encysted would still be subjective things, varying with the personal observations of each biologist. Disagreements as to the respiration or even the heart-beat of a certain patient would be just as subjective, or variant, among doctors, were it not for the exact measurements of the stethoscope. It is only an accepted system of coördinates, then, that can make possible exactness of comparison, or, in other terms, objective scientific knowledge.

The advance of science will be determined by its ability to get all objects down to an objective basis. The main purpose of science is to be able to predict; given the object and the receptor it must aim to reach the point where it can predict the reaction. It can do that now with many of the reactions of matter; with each addition to its knowledge it approaches closer to its goal. It must be admitted that measurement itself is a premise, but it is a premise accepted by all because of its inevitability. It is possible, to be vexingly onto-logical for the moment, that both form and substance are illusions. But working from a realist or materialist basis, which is the only scientific and logical one, meas-urement by exact coördinates is the only route that science can follow.

Of all things that have caused befuddlement and confusion, and that have made psychology unable to get to an objective basis, the term "consciousness" is supreme. There have been more definings of that term than any other, and, to quote Engel's ingenious phras-ing, since "each one's special (definition) is again conditioned by his subjective understanding, his con-ditions of existence, the measure of his knowledge and his intellectual training, there is no other ending pos-sible in this conflict of (definitions) than that they shall all be mutually exclusive of the others."

There is the naïve conception of consciousness that things in the mind are exact replicas of reality; the dualist conception of two worlds, the mental and the physical, and that consciousness, obviously consisting only of the mental, has a different picture of things than they really are; the critical realist conception; the idealist conception; the solipsistic, etc.; all staunchly maintained by their respective advocates, and each with its own peculiar logic. None can be said to be positively wrong since there is no way to get definite knowledge of what consciousness is, that is, providing we assume it to exist in the fashion that the usual metaphysician does. It may be a thing existing in all cells, as some have maintained, or a thing—what a vague word!—peculiar only to the cerebral cortex as Gall first pointed out, and as most physiologists and psychologists now contend. At any rate, it is a thing as unmeasurable almost as the first cause, and pursuing the road psychology has trodden from the time of Aristotle to that of Titchener, that is, the introspective, it will get no closer to objective knowledge than it had got at the time of John Locke.

Moreover, since consciousness itself is but the product of stimuli, and since, to follow radical determinist psychology, all thought is determined or reflex, consciousness is but the coördinate center of nervous impulses, and needs to be given no more consideration than is given the usual heart-beat or rhythmical segmentation of the intestinal system. Since consciousness does not control behavior it is a fallacy to magnify it into a bugaboo barrier. To use Watson's figure, consciousness is merely the shadow of leaves upon the ground. It receives and transmits impulses, interfering in no particular. Consciousness is caused by the same thing that causes behavior, namely, the functioning of the nervous system.

Behavior, on the other hand, can be observed and measured. In this way we can come to exactness, to scientific method. By this means psychology can become a science, and defy Comte's dictum. Notwithstanding how real an object is, no scientific examination and criticism of it are possible until a definite system of coördinates is accepted.

The psychology that at present is pursuing the scientific method indicated in this article, the only method possible if psychology is ever to be founded on a basis as objective as that of physical science, is commonly known as behaviorism. It is necessary to remark here that hints of the behaviorist method, with actual attempts in that direction, are to be discovered in many of the various texts on psychology and philosophy that were written during the last three centuries. Perhaps the most striking of these was that made by Johann Nicholas Tetens, who in his *Philosophische Versuche* (1777) endeavored to found an independent psychology which should be entirely based on observation and experiment. Tetens, in the beginning, attempted the measurement of images produced by different sensations, but later veered sadly from the materialist method. Behaviorism is a philosophy as well as a psychology, notwithstanding the devout attempts of some behaviorists to avoid anything like philosophic concepts. It is a scientific philosophy, if you will. Carried to its legitimate limits it is a mechanist philosophy, that bases all of its conclusions upon observation and experiment. It carefully and meticulously avoids all voluntarist metaphysics. It eschews any reference to "consciousness" or a "conscious process." Sufficient reasons were given above for this. Any mention of an *élan vital* is obviously taboo. A stimulus-response psychology, as it has been frequently described, views all action as a response to stimulation—a response is the total striped and unstriped muscular and glandular activity that occurs as a result of stimulation. A brain never gets into action save through a sense organ; it is necessary to note here that every muscle besides being an effector is also a sense organ. An emotion is an inherited "pattern-reaction" involving profound changes of the bodily mechanism as a whole, but particularly of the visceral and glandular systems. Emotion appears at times of emergency. It is the organization of visceral activity in an emotion that tends to give the additional drive and energy to the body—the blood pressure, for instance, is raised and the blood tends to coagulate. Emotion and instinct are differentiated by patent variations in be-

[255]

havior.[1] The shock of an emotional stimulus throws the organism, for the moment at least, into a chaotic state, and during that moment it can make few adjustments to its environment; in the case of instinct, which involves the striped muscles, that indecision and chaos do not result, and, minus the diffuseness of an emotion, the action is specific and definitized. In specific activity, or instinct, you have little if any visceral involvement; in diffuse, at any rate less specific, activity, or emotion, you have unmistakable visceral involvements. All activity is fundamentally the result of visceral drive. The energy one embodies, for instance, is derived from persistent stimulation in the viscera; any type of activity tends, according to its vigor and pertinence, to reduce this tension, temporarily if the activity is temporary, constantly if the activity is constant. Those kinds of activity that reduce the drive immediately are those that remove the stimulus. The conditioned reflex is used to explain the origin and persistence of habit. Mental abnormalities raise no insolvable difficulties for the behaviorist. Diseased personality arises from habit distortion. Manic-Depressive psychosis, for example, is explained as the result of the advent of certain chemical (glandular) sub-

[1] It is important to note here that Professor J. B. Watson, the originator of modern behaviorism, and the psychologist who has undoubtedly made the most important contribution to American psychology, uses entirely the genetic method in his discovery and analysis of emotions and instincts.

stances into the blood; in dementia præcox cases, where you discover certain tension, the hand-resting having a different appearance from normal and the arm being incapable of elevation without great tenseness, you have an absence of adrenalin in the blood, or some other chemical element, which closes a number of the synapses and prevents free and nonantagonistic muscular activity.[2] It is in the matter of thought that behaviorism takes its most revolutionary stand. Thought occurs where a problem opens and visceral tension persists; it is purely cœnæsthetic, each thought following the other in purely muscular manner. Thought, then, is a form of behavior, consisting of subvocal movements of speech muscles; every thought, therefore, must have a physiological corollary to determine it. Speech is a form of substitute behavior; speech movements are associated with ordinary movements and are thoroughly muscular in character. Speech, a direct method of lessening visceral tension, is reduced to a minimum as habits become established. Merely unpleasant speech behavior is eliminated in the case of repressions.

[2] In the matter of sex, it should be observed, behaviorists are quite Freudian in their interpretations. Wherever an organism makes a positive reaction towards an object it is because the object stimulates its erogenous zones, causing a state of tumescence (the individual in many cases is not aware of this)—the erogenous zones are the sex organs proper and any other tissues that become rigid—and whenever it makes a negative reaction it is because the object stimulates detumescence. Smoking, for illustration, affords pleasure because it stimulates the erogenous tissue, the lips, to a state of temporary tumescence.

[257]

In brief, then, the examination of all reaction should be confined to physical methods, since they alone, based already upon accepted coördinates, can give objective knowledge, and explanation of it should be made entirely in physical terms.

That the whole philosophy underlying this objective psychology, so maligned often under the name of behaviorism, has crying and significant social meanings is too little appreciated even by its warmest advocates. It is the wicked tendency of the specialist, be he a physicist, geologist, histologist, or psychologist, to narrow his observations to the laboratory and limit his conclusions to his immediate science. In the fashion that the old historians devoted themselves to the mere discovery and narration of fact, the modern scientists too frequently venture no coördination of data that extend beyond the confined scope of their particular inquiry. Induction, as a method, is fruitless unless general conclusions of importance can be derived from the collected facts. The social philosophy of behaviorism has yet to be written. In a sentence, it is cause and effect psychology reduced to its lowest common denominator. This at once implies a deterministic interpretation of individual and social activity. With this arise the problems that surround the question of "morals and determinism," which frightened Renouvier long before Professor Jastrow. Since no response is possible without a stimulus, all of man's actions must be viewed as determined by the stimuli that come to him, that is, determined by the kind of environment in which he lives. As Professor Watson indicated, could the son of a Pharaoh at birth he removed across time and space and be reared along with other lads in Boston, it lies well within the range of probability that he would develop into the same kind of college youth that we find among other Harvard students; his reactions to situations, notwithstanding the difference in his ancestry, would be approximately the same as those of a native New England boy, and "his chance for success in life would probably not be at all different from those of his classmates." It is change of environment, or change of stimulus in simpler terms, that will bring about change in reaction. As a social philosophy the significance of this can readily be seen. Man, as La Mettrie accurately saw him, a reaction-machine, behaves differently, and better, in a good environment than in a bad, just as he is healthier in a sanitary environment than in an unsanitary. If the theory of evolution be correct, whatever we call heredity must at one time have come from environment, and must have been changed as environmental influences demanded, and must continue to be changed in this same way as long as life survives. In other words, since heredity must be a product of environment, it must be changed no matter how gradually or swiftly, whenever the environment is changed. No intelligent doctor will deny that if you change a baby's unhealthful environment to a healthful one, and continue the latter throughout his life, no predispositions to disease that he may have inherited will be given opportunity to develop. By an extensive change in environment, therefore, the method of an accurate social psychology, and not by selective interbreeding and cries for the *"Uebermensch,"* will an improved race be created. The details as to all of these changes have certainly not been *all* discovered. It is the purpose, however, and fundamental value, of an objective psychology to work toward an objective sociology.

ART, SCIENCE AND THE QUANTITATIVE
CONCEPTION

THAT "all things are numbers," the Pythagorean conception, arising from application of limit to the unlimited, is ridiculously uninspiring to the mind of the modern age. The significance of the attempt of the Pythagoreans to define Justice as a square number is entirely uncomprehended. Yet these Greek metaphysicians were on the right track, however little their direction may have been understood. To change the Protagorean declaration into a Pythagorean: "Number is the measure of all things." Number limits and reduces substance to a quantitative basis. There is, of course, the Platonic separatism to be noted, that numbers themselves are unique forms, universal in their sense of application, but "inaddible" as mere numbers unless considered in reference to definite objects. As Plato showed, if we say that "seven and six are thirteen," we mean that seven units of a certain kind added to six units of the same kind equal thirteen units of that kind, but not that the number seven added to the number six equals the number thirteen. The numbers in themselves are patently inaddible. When applied to objects, however, which is their function, numbers become the means of computation and exactitude. They give the quantitative characteristic to our universe. They become the means of discovering and designating the relationship of objects, the precise nature of their structure and movement, and, to a degree, of controlling their future evolution and change.

Why do numbers have these attributes? these advantages? Because they have a definiteness of denotation that is unobscured by emotional preference or rationalization. Because of their objectivity of meaning and value they afford a fundamental basis for comparison. They can indicate the separateness of objects and also their synthesis. Their purpose—to limit—is in itself well-nigh illimitable.

We can conceive of nothing in nature that cannot be reduced to number. If a thing is,[1] then it has quantity and that quantity has numerical character. To speak of an object in space is but to state that it has length, breadth, and thickness. Can we conceive of length, breadth, and thickness aside from number? Such an act is clearly fatuous. Infinitudes and infinitesimals do not escape the quantitative symbol. An electron cannot exist unless we can give it attributes, and attributes resolve themselves into states of matter

---

[1] By is, in this reference, we mean is for us. It is possible for many things to be that we cannot perceive and know, but for us they do not exist.

and motion, problems of mass and velocity, measurement, and number. We speak of points in space, of imaginary centers, infinitesimal nuclei, of electrical force, and yet we invariably give these hypothetic entities quantitative character in terms of the forces that made necessary their postulation. It is impossible to escape this circle of demarcation.

The trend of modern science is to reduce the qualitative to the quantitative—to reduce all substance to a quantitative basis. To limit the entire universe by number. This is the path the human mind must pursue if it is to get its knowledge upon an objective level. The external universe has come within our ken, so to speak, with our ability to deal with its varying aspects in an objective manner; description must lead into classification and classification into generalization, the ultimate end of science, if progress is to be made, and classification and generalization are impossible without an established, indisputably accepted series of coördinates. The attempts of Russell to construct a system of symbolic logic, for instance, are evidences of the desire to get to objectivity through a means more satisfactory than words. With numbers controversies begin to cease. Attributes, then, can be noted with quantitative exactitude and motion described with objective accuracy.

Were it not for our reduction of the physical universe to a quantitative basis, the physical sciences could never have flourished. Let us for a moment scissor more deeply into the problem of the qualitative and the quantitative. The quantitative quite obviously represents those characteristics of substance that can be expressed by number: weight, compressibility, expansibility, length, breadth, thickness. And what is the qualitative of which we have so much discussion and to which we have so much reference? How can we explain or define it? Let us for a moment retreat to the dictionary. "That from the possession of which anything is such as it is; the element, form, or mode of being or action of anything which seems to make it distinct from other things; distinguishing character; essential property": such are the sundry definitions of quality. "Having to do with qualities only; relating to differences or distinctions in kind as opposed to differences in quantity," such the definitions of qualitative. Quantity, as we said, has to deal with number, amount. "Having distinctions of (amount) rather than kind or character; the state or condition of being so much; magnitude, size, amount, number; the property of a thing which admits of exact measurement." The last definition is of great significance. It distinguishes, in a more philosophic sense than is at first realized, the quantitative from the qualitative. From the above definitions it is clear that the qualitative is the unmeasurable, that which has not been, or seemingly cannot be, reduced to number.

But what can we mean when we say that the trend of science is toward the reduction of the qualitative to the quantitative? Again we shall recline upon an illustration. This time we shall employ the concept of color. .Now what do we discover when we begin to examine this concept? First, we find that there are different colors: red, green, yellow, and other hues of the spectrum; and secondly, that these colors may appear in varying forms, in picture-space or in skyey panorama. In either form the two attributes are present. The differences between the colors, the designations of red, green, orange, and the like are the qualitative; the differences in form, in numerical size, length and breadth, are the quantitative. This division at one time seemed unchangeable, final. Now, although the verbal qualifiers still linger, we shall see how modern science has resolved the qualitative into the quantitative and thus marked a revolution in human thought. Thought, to have social significance, must have that definiteness and precision necessary for its conveyance, with a minimal chance of error, to other minds. The quantitative characteristics permit this conveyance with most success. In the case of color the qualitative attributes, red, orange, blue, can now be expressed in terms of wave-lengths, quantitatively. Instead of speaking of the color red we can speak of the range of wave-lengths between 7,600 Angstroms and 6,400 Angstroms, which not only signifies the color but also indicates with exactitude its degree of proximity to the other colors on the chromatic scale. We thus are able to resolve qualitative distinctions to a quantitative basis. The color blue becomes equivalent to 4,600 to 4,300; green to 5,500 to 4,700; yellow to 5,900 to 5,500. The formerly unmeasurable becomes measurable.

Reducing substance to the quantitative is tantamount to reducing it to its lowest common denominator. We distinguish certain types of glass from certain types of diamonds not by their respective fascination for the eye, but by their quantitative disparities. In fact all of our distinctions of the qualitative are but admissions of inexactitude, of our incapacity to reduce substance to the primary concepts of measurement. Our qualifiers, our variety of adjectives and adverbs,— what are they but clear manifestations of this incapacity? Rich, as a rich play; severe, as a severe pain; soft, as a soft sound; elegant; fine; splendid—we could name hundreds—what are these but expressions of vagueness, painful indefiniteness? *Until these can be reduced to definite quantitative character they are entirely unworkable forms from the point of view of science.* Their meaning now is as varied and oscillating

[266]

as the confusing bursts of a cyclone. Suppose we indicate another example directly in line with our analysis
that further reveals the "qualitative to quantitative"
reductive tendency. There was a time when diagnosis
of renal colic due to a stone had to be described by
the patient in terms of "severe," "aching," "mild," "ex-
cruciating," "compressing"—extremely vague indices
of sensation and activity; while now, since the invention of the cystoscope, we can determine the exact location of the stone, determine the relative efficiency of
the kidneys; and with the aid of the X-ray even the
exact position of the kidneys can be ascertained; so
that description in terms of the qualitative, adjectives
and gestures, is supplanted by exact analysis in terms
of the quantitative. With the eye, the opthalmoscope,
an instrument able to measure the least pathologic
change in the optic nerve or choroid, has achieved a
similar exactitude. By means of the stomach tube we
are able to trace digestion in the stomach from the moment of the entrance of food to the moment of its dis-
charge, and through the X-ray we can follow changes
in the motility of the stomach and localize disease.
Without the cystoscope, X-ray, ureometer and the like,
methods of the quantitative, medical diagnosis would
still be floundering in a mist of conjecture. And again,
if we take instruments like the audiometer we discover
a quantitative method for determining the exact degree

of loss of hearing, the loss being given in the form of percentage. The illuminometer, to give another illustration, an instrument for accurately calculating the intensity of light expressed in candle power per square foot, has reduced the problem of the effect of light from a qualitative to a quantitative basis. The mere listing of the machines that have been devised by scientists in an attempt to reduce the qualitative to the quantitative—the optical pyrometer, spinthariscope, penetrometer, adhesivometer, polariscope, etc.—is scarcely necessary to prove a point so incontestably patent. It should not be forgotten also that there was a time when we spoke of infinitesimals in terms of the qualitative, one-hundred-thousandths of an inch became "indescribably small" units—now by electrical method we can measure one-millionth of an inch and can observe by optical method a change of position of approximately the same order of magnitude. To further illustrate our advance in quantitative method, we can now detect in electrical current the passage of a single electron, the ultimate unit of electricity, and its track, composed of the wreckage of atoms it has caused, can be photographed. Time intervals, for instance, can be handled down to one-four-hundred-millionth of a second. These are but further examples of the definiteness and advance of the quantitative approach.

Let us take a usual differentiation between quality and quantity and point out its superficiality and falsity. Quality is better than quantity, a small thing of precious character is superior to a large thing of unprecious character! Such is heard from one end of the world to the other. Now this differentiation, though true in one sense, is fundamentally a misconception of the genuine character of quantity. *Quantity, as we showed before, is merely the measurable element.* It is not only concerned with length, breadth, and thickness, but any and all elements that are measurable. In the small object it is possible at times, that, though we have less quantity in the sense of length, breadth, and thickness, we have more quantity in the subtler elements of the substance. The difference, in a last analysis, therefore, is a quantitative one just the same. A diamond drill is superior to a steel drill not because it is smaller in size or, to employ the usual distinction, because it is of finer quality—this may be true but it is deplorably and unworkably vague—but because of the quantitative differences of resistance to pressure and capacity to cut. These differences of resistance and capacity to cut are quantitative, or rather the formerly qualitative differences are sifted down to the quantitative. The smaller object in the instance above, though it has less of what is usually called quantity, mass, and density and the like, has quantitative superiority in other char-

[269]

acteristics. Some of these characteristics as yet may not be measured; in fact, we may not be able to measure some of them at the present time, but that they will finally be reduced to a quantitative basis is surely not part of an inconceivable proposition. It is just this function in which science excels. There is a difference between chasing the objective and chasing the rainbow.

Just as we now can distinguish types of vision by the quantitative method, differences of focus and intensity, it is the aim of science to distinguish all of the varying shades of response. To declare that the ultimate achievement of such an end must be relegated to a future dimmed by remoteness is not to disparage the value of the method. It is only the quantitative, the measurable resemblances and differences, the computable theses, antitheses, and syntheses, that leads to objectivity of knowledge, and without this objectivity thought must remain groping in a mystical Valhalla. The human mind, attracted by the infinite, deceived by the immediate, has been fearful of final exactitude. The mysterious, the undefined, the magic of the unknown, have been haunting *ignes fatui*. To the artist and the voluntarist metaphysician they are the embodiment of the sublime, the source of the exquisite. Man the unpredictable, the free, empyrean spirit, the unfathomable soul, is the ideal of the artist, the inspiration of his genius; man the predictable, the limited, deter-

[270]

mined organism, the mechanistic creation of material forces, is death to him, the atrophy and annihilation of his impulse—thus has reasoned the artist and esthetician of past centuries and today. To apply number to his art is to scourge it of beauty. The qualitative, the unmeasurable, fascinates him; the quantitative, the measurable, repels him. Yet it is this very application of number that instead of deadening will eventually rejuvenate art. To reduce an object, even a feeling, to a quantitative basis is not to injure or depreciate its value. By discovering precision of attribute an object becomes a more complete reality and the opportunity of enhancing its beauty is increased. Its origin, modes of change, relationship to other objects, temporal and spatial relativity, become more clarified as the process of quantitative analysis approaches a successful conclusion. With this knowledge the object naturally comes more under our control and we are able to accentuate, by increase in quantitative proportions, those attributes that please and obscure or eliminate those that pain. The success with which medicine is able to avoid certain phases of pain-activity by the ability to gauge and predict in quantitative fashion those physiological changes consequent from certain stimuli is important from a hedonistic as well as health-giving point of view. There was a time too when the application of quantitative methods to the human body seemed an egregious sacrilege, when the thought that bodily action was mechanistic was parlous heterodoxy inspiring of persecution. Today we recognize that without such approach the problems of human reaction would have been as obscure as they were in the days preceding Vesalius and Harvey. The attitude of the artist and esthetician of today—and that of the vitalist, in fact the whole Voluntarist school—is analogous to that of the average physician of the day before yesterday—the day when the Scots forbade medical attendance to a boil for fear that the purpose of God might be frustrated as a result, and the Spanish professors maintained that cleaning the streets would deprive the air of the bad smells that rendered it uninjurious.

It is the concept of number, the source of the quantitative, therefore, that must be applied and extended with more intelligent emphasis. It is the *sine qua non* of objectivity. We devise apparatus, invent machines, in order to attain this objectivity of measurement and calculation. The tendency to emotional preference— purely wavering, qualitative distinctions—in this way is avoided. It is necessary to reiterate at this point that the only hope science has of becoming inclusive of all phenomena is by reducing the qualitative to the quantitative, reducing the now unmeasurable to the measurable. The growth of the physical sciences is but the history of this evolution. In the social sciences, economics, psychology, and sociology are all driving in that direction. The investigations of Ferri in criminology, the rise of the behaviorist movement in psychology, are plain and inescapable evidences of how the students of social and mental science have realized that the qualitative must be reduced to the quantitative if their work is to attain objectivity and be assured of permanent progress.

This evolution marks the significant transition from the ethical to the scientific method. Science is concerned with truth, "the correspondence between idea and reality," not with good and bad; the "accuracy of a truth is to be determined by the accuracy of this correspondence," not by the pleasure or pain it affords. From the qualitative method spring ethical controversies which the quantitative eliminates through its unquestioning exactitude. The aim of the latter, in sociology, for instance, is to reduce the entirety of social phenomena to a quantitative basis whereby we can calculate origins and change, and predict results from given forces. It will ultimately mean the reduction of sociology to number.[2] This further will change the controversies over social goods and bads into issues of the quantitative. It is true that the achievement of

[2] The work of Quetelet, the Belgian, for example, was a beginning in this direction.

[273]

this end may lie "beyond the horizon," but the means of crossing the distance is coming rapidly within our control.

It is important to note here also that there is no attempt to state that "number" solves the problem of reality, that with its application the enigmas of epistemology vanish and the difficulties of life and death lose their tormenting perplexity and unanswerability. This would be quixotic fatuity. We do not disagree with Eddington—nor with Kant—that number leaves the *ding an sich* unsolved, that "this knowledge is only an empty shell—a form of symbols. It is knowledge of structural form, and not knowledge of content. All through the physical world runs that unknown content, which must surely be the stuff of consciousness."[3]

Keplerian discoveries, however vast and significant as generalizations, do not dispose of the quandaries of teleology. The unfathomable "whys and wherefores" that drove the sad Omar to drink are not shot into oblivion by the idea of scientific progression. Their solutions must be reserved for the vagaries of the ontologist, the futilities of the metaphysician. Science, working from the law of cause and effect, inductively collecting, culling and categorizing, can offer description and explanation only in terms of structural form, quantitative character; the moment it attempts to de-

[3] A. J. Eddington—*Space, Time and Gravitation.*

scribe and explain *content* as distinct from form, the origin of matter, the stuff that beyond the ions and electrons reality actually *is,* it automatically becomes unscientific and metaphysical. Its objectivity is immediately destroyed.

Yet it is precisely this mastery over form, this knowledge of structure, which number, the quantitative method, science, gives, that has made possible our boundarizing of the universe and its activity and from which has sprung our ability to compare, classify, and predict with accuracy. With Hegel we are prone to agree that to know all of the properties of an object is for practical purposes all that we need to know, and as a necessary expedient therefore we can afford to discard, or shall we say neglect, the *ding an sich.* It would be excessive folly to claim that number can ever account for every change in the endless flux of the universe, the interpretation of each electron and impulse, and fix their structure and motion as one would impale a stick—such would be to make movement static, an absurdity in itself. But that number can render this universal process more intelligible, give it the objective character necessary for our working with it, goes without question. When an object can be reduced to number it becomes a definite form. This is what science is working towards, what scientific philosophy must set as its goal. If states of fatigue can be spoken of in terms of number instead of "intense" or "mild," if in time, despite their bewildering multiplicities of origin and expression, emotions can be designated in a manner similarly objective, we shall be on the road to a realization of this end in the reactions of the human organism—as firmly indeed as we now are in the reactions of the physical world. It will mean a "quantitating" of the universe, a reduction of the qualitative to the quantitative, a revolutionary progression in approach and conclusion.

REFLECTIONS ON THE TREND OF MODERN PSYCHOLOGY AS EXEMPLIFIED BY FOUR PSYCHOLOGISTS

OF all sciences the most significant must necessarily be sociology. An accurate sociology will depend upon an accurate conception of the individual and environment. Misconception of either will distort and injure whatever illations are drawn from the data presented. Misconceptions arise from either insufficiency of facts or from hasty and incorrect coördination of them. Sociological conceptions are dependent upon the facts derived from every science, and the effectiveness and value of every science are dependent upon its capacity to draw from its facts, in relation to the facts of other sciences, accurate sociological conclusions. The individual sciences, at the present time, in large part, are in a state of isolation and anarchy. The physicist refrains from carrying his investigation into the science of chemistry, and the chemist in turn will not hazard investigation into physics, with the result that there exist a physical conception of the structure of matter, of the nature and operations of the electron, and a chemical conception. The physiologist will discuss neuron-patterns, reflex arcs, the sensitivity of an organism to stimuli, the physical and chemical nature of reaction, and yet, although he admits the dependence of mind on body, will hesitate to extend his conclusions on physiology into an explanation of psychological response.[1] The psychologist will elucidate mental response, but avoid examination of motive and the resolution of it into its primary and inevitable causes.

In Kempf's *Psychopathology,* for instance, illustration of this attitude of psychologists can be clearly observed. The volume is one of fascinating description and clever analysis. The cases presented furnish evidence sufficient for a number of safe and correct generalizations. The approach is scientific, though the conclusions lack both precision and comprehensiveness. The organism is studied as an object capable of certain forms of behavior, all of which are determined by the nature of the stimulus and the capacity of the organism to respond to it. Existence is a matter of adjustment. The parallelistic issues of consciousness are avoided by scientific analysis. Kempf's position, in this respect, is distinctly "behavioristic." Consciousness and the content of consciousness, he maintains, are but the "reaction of the body as a unity to the sensational activity of one or several of its parts." The Freudian censor and the concepts of "egoistic unity," "segmental

[1] See Howell's *A Textbook of Physiology,* 8th edition, pages 148, 149.

cravings" and the like, are given clear and satisfactory exposition. The work of Sherrington, Cannon, Pawlow, and Bechterew is used as a basis for all the psychological deductions that follow. There is, as a consequence, no sentimental "freudianizing." The important contributions of the psychoanalyst school, particularly those of Freud, Jung, Adler and Bleuler, however, are in no way underestimated.

It has been Kempf's work on the autonomic system, of course, that has been most singular and significant. He has extended the physiological observations and discoveries of the operation of the autonomic apparatus made by Pawlow, Watson, and Bechterew into the psychological plane, and attempted to construct, from the evidence at hand, a genuine biological psychiatry. This is his step in advance. And it is the only step that can be made if psychiatry is to attain the objectivity of a science.

It is in his sociological conclusions that we find Kempf doing the stunt of the sciolist. It is the stunt that is performed daily by scientists of every degree. While a scientist would hesitate to make a conclusion in his particular science without first giving careful study to his object and to the collection of his evidence, in the matter of sociology he will hazard an inference without trepidation, his ignorance of sociological factors notwithstanding. If his specialty be sex-psychology, his

[279]

conclusion will be concerned solely with sex-reform. If he be a nutritionist, dietetics is the method to social regeneration. And so it is with Kempf. He suddenly comes to the conclusion that we should "seriously doubt the fitness of the present educational system and its puritanic ideals, the present expositions of religion and social law, and of the average parent to train a child," and believes that he has gotten to the root of individual and social disorganization. Tendencies to exhibitionism alarm him, and the danger of biological castration sends him into a long tirade against instruction by non-reproductive and homo-sexual teachers. Like the spiritistic McDougall he childishly indulges in the fear that sterilization of the upper strata may force the heritage of the American continent into the hands of "the more primitive European immigrant." In other words, he has no conception of historical progress, of the telluric and economic forces that determine individual and social action, that decide and shape customs, prejudices, and ideas. Nor does he realize that it is only by complete change of environment, which will come with the next evolution in society, that even such minor changes as he desires and advocates can be accomplished. As a psychologist he is a scientist, as a sociologist he is an utopian. As a scientist he is significant, as an utopian he merits little consideration.

In Hunter's *General Psychology* we meet with a

textbook that pretends to nothing new except method of presentation. In this respect it is interesting and possesses certain pedagogical value. It is in definite opposition to the "functionalism" of the older psychology which we still see propounded in the tomes of a number of contemporary psychologists. On the other hand, it attempts to felicitously coördinate the theories of behaviorism and structuralism, a task quite Sisyphean in character. As an elementary text, however, a book to be studied in classroom, it has a simplicity of style and a clarity of exposition that make it distinctly superior to such books as Dunlap's *A System of Psychology*, Breese's *Psychology*, Titchener's *Textbook on Psychology*, or Calkin's *A First Book in Psychology*, books all devised for the same purpose. In its sociological conclusions, nevertheless, its references to environment, fundamental causes of neuroses, the Kallikak family and the like, it is no more comprehensive or satisfactory than Kempf.

Robinson and Robinson's *Readings in General Psychology* introduces us to a valuable collection of psychological material. It is likewise a textbook, written with the laudable purpose, however, of providing the student with easy access to the developments in psychological theory and experiment. The labors of the two Robinsons are to be commended. Such a book as this fills an important need, particularly for the student or lay reader who is too occupied with other tasks to find time to search for his information through psychological journals, reviews, and textbooks. It would have been more in accord with the trend of recent psychological advance to have devoted greater space to the discoveries and theories of the behaviorist school, and more stimulating to the student to have included selections from Ferenzi, Pfister, Jung, and even the Americans, Jelliffe, McCurdy, Frink, and Sidis. Of course, we could not expect good selections of social psychology (although the title *Readings in General P. ...logy* should include it) where, as we have indicated, no accurate social psychology exists.

Mechanism, Life and Personality presents an interesting contrast to all of the other books that we have discussed. Science is here given a philosophic evaluation. In the first and most brilliant essay in the volume, *The Mechanistic Theory of Life,* Haldane skilfully analyzes the vitalist hypothesis and clearly shows its insupportability. In the later essays his attack is less certain and accurate. He is more deeply concerned with the problem of philosophic fiction, however, than the general scientist, and even goes so far as to predict that, in time, with the progress of knowledge, "matter will be recognized as nothing but an appearance." Notwithstanding his attack upon vitalism, he objects to the realist hypothesis that the world is something self-existent and outside of us, because it drives us to admit that all that we can immediately perceive are sensory disturbances, and as a result our conception of the world can be nothing more than a stream of sensations, a serial phantasmagoria formed according to the manner in which our sensations group themselves. The inadequacy of the mechanistic theory arises from its necessary assumption that the world is a reality existing outside of us, and that its substance and motion can be reduced to scientific formulæ. Science can deal only with partial and incomplete aspects of reality; it is the "application of abstract logical principles to a reality which they can never express fully." Yet Lord Haldane uses the same logical abstractions to reveal the illogicality of scientific logic. Where one must use the same instruments he attacks, he must be exceedingly cautious as to their application. The significance of this the author has not seemed to realize. The conclusion that "spiritual reality is the only reality and from this point of view philosophy and religion are one," is unfortunately the one that we must expect from the voluntarist, utopian type of mind.

No science can lay claim to finality of judgment, nor can any poetic or metaphysical system. To maintain that the world in the mind is nothing more than a complex of sensory disturbances does not invalidate the conclusions drawn from them. So long as everyone experiences approximately similar sensory disturbances, we are at least in a position to affirm or deny the objectivity of a piece of knowledge, according as it can or cannot be perceived by others similarly equipped. Whatever the *ding an sich*, assuming its existence, or the final nature of perception and awareness, whether it be real or illusory, this conclusion remains unassailable. And upon it depends the truth and development of science.

THE END